Dictionary of Latin American Spanish
Phrases and Expressions

Dictionary of Latin American Spanish
Phrases and Expressions

Eleanor Hamer and
Fernando Díez de Urdanivia

HIPPOCRENE BOOKS
NEW YORK

ISBN 0-7818-0865-0

For information, address:
Hippocrene Books, Inc.
171 Madison Avenue
New York, NY 10016

Library of Congress Cataloging-in-Publication Data

Hamer, Eleanor.
 Dictionary of Latin American Spanish phrases and expressions / Nina
 Hamer and Fernando Díez de Urdanivia.
   p.cm.
 Includes index.
 ISBN 0-7818-0865-0
 1. Spanish language—Provincialisms—Latin America—Dictionaries. 2.
 Spanish language—Dictionaries—English. I. Díez de Urdanivia,
 Fernando. II. Title.

 PC4822 .H36 2001
 467' .98—dc21

                                                           2001039542

Jacket and book design by Acme Klong Design, Inc.

Printed in the United States of America.

Table of Contents

About This Book

There is no task more difficult than compiling a dictionary. From the many-tomed encyclopedia to the pocket phrase book, it is always a challenge. A glance at any of them suffices to reveal their shortcomings, and sometimes their errors, which is why every dictionary should come equipped with a few words of introduction to put the reader on guard against any ill-conceived ideas of perfection.

This is a basic dictionary. Any attempt at covering the Spanish of Latin America in its entirety would be more or less unachievable, and in any case, would fill a considerable number of volumes.

This book, however, will be very helpful for English-speaking persons studying Spanish or traveling south of the Rio Grande (Río Bravo in Spanish), since it contains the bulk of the everyday expressions used in Latin America. Also included are words with a meaning that is either different or in addition to the meaning found in regular dictionaries.

The origins of each expression are provided, and when applicable, the various meanings or ways that each expression is used in the different areas of Latin America. When no notations are given, this signifies that the expression is used in almost all countries, although care should be taken with possible nuances of distinction. Colloquial language in Latin America, as elsewhere in the world, changes from country to country and from one area to another within the same country. Usage can also vary from one section of a city to another, and sometimes even among families in any given portion of a city. It simply is not possible to indicate such variations in a dictionary of this size.

Almost none of the expressions in this book that are common to all countries of Latin America are used in their literal sense. There are exceptions that, although likely to be found in an ordinary dictionary, form part of overall Latin American colloquialisms. Many entries do also include the literal meaning, which can be quite delightful. In addition, examples have been provided for many of the expressions, with their equivalent English expression. For entries with no example, the translation will suffice to get the idea across. Please note that an equivalent expression is not always available in the other language to convey the meaning. In those cases, a plain explanation has been provided.

Part of speech is provided for the Spanish entries, while slang and vulgar terms are marked as such in both the Spanish and English sections. Obscene terms have been omitted, not entirely due to moral considerations. There are many of these expressions that no one would think anything of in one country, yet may be taboo elsewhere. The reader will find some examples of this type of dichotomy and these can serve as a basis for interpreting many of the objectionable terms not included in this book.

The book consists of two sections. The first: *Phrases and Expressions in Spanish*, is ordered according to the Spanish alphabet. Words which appear in parentheses are not taken into alphabetical consideration. The second section: *Phrases and Expressions in English*, offers the Spanish equivalent for a selection of English expressions. When pertinent, multiple translations, origins of Spanish expressions, and examples of English usage, with one or more parallel Spanish translations, are included. This section is ordered according to the English alphabet. The "to" preceding an infinitive is not taken into alphabetical consideration. Additionally, the index offers a quick reference to the more than 1,400 expressions found in this collection.

If this book is helpful to the student or traveler, and if it provides a means of shedding light on the linguistic gems of present-day Spanish, we will consider our mission accomplished.

Abbreviations Used in this Book

adj.	adjective/adjectival phrase
adv.	adverb/adverbial phrase
aff.	affirmative
Arg	Argentina
Bol	Bolivia
CA	Central America
Chi	Chile
Col	Colombia
CR	Costa Rica
DR	Dominican Republic
Ecu	Ecuador
ES	El Salvador
Gua	Guatemala
Hon	Honduras
lit.	literally
Mex	Mexico
n.	noun
neg.	negative
Pana	Panama
Para	Paraguay
PR	Puerto Rico
pron.	pronoun
Uru	Uruguay
v.	verb/verbal phrase
Ven	Venezuela

About the Authors

Born in Mexico to a British family, **ELEANOR HAMER**'s professional life began in Lima, Peru where she taught English as a second language for four years at the Instituto Peruano-Norteamericano and the Universidad de Lima. She then moved back to Mexico, where she was made Director of the Insurgentes branch of the Berlitz School of Languages in Mexico City after teaching there for only a month. A short time later, she became independent, and directed and co-owned Pennington Cultural Center. She then became director of the language laboratory at Ingenieros Civiles Asociados (where she took three years to write her first course of English as a second language), and eventually (in 1975) she became sole owner of Hamersharp (English as a second language for business executives), for which she developed the definitive (and very effective) course (ten textbooks for the student and ten teacher manuals, used very successfully at the Hamersharp schools to this date) as well as *Writing Business English* for the most advanced students. Her aversion to administrative work led her to give up running Hamersharp, and for the last fourteen years, she has been the official translator for Price Waterhouse (now PricewaterhouseCoopers) in Mexico City.

FERNANDO DÍEZ DE URDANIVIA is a graduate of the Carlos Septién García school of journalism in Mexico. The son of a prominent Mexican journalist, he has written for *Excélsior, Novedades, El Heraldo de México, El Día* and *El Universal*, and was one of the founders of *El Diario de la Tarde de Novedades*. For many years he wrote for a wide variety of Mexican magazines (including *Hoy, Abside* and *Sembradores*). In 1998 he was awarded the National Journalism Prize for his interviewing work.

He has taught Spanish composition and literature at the Escuela Carlos Septién García, the Universidad Motolinía, the Centro de Estudios of the University of California in Mexico, the Chicano Studies Center of Santa Barbara, California in Mexico, and the Instituto Cultural Hispano Mexicano, and was Director of the Centro de Estudios Periodísticos. Aside from that, he has taught many literary and creative writing workshops.

His published works include *The Spanish Game* (with Luisa María Alvarez), *Mi Historia Secreta de la Música, Cómo Hablan los que Escriben* (interviews with famous writers), *Te doy mi Palabra de Amor, Sabiduría en Pocas Líneas* and *En el Umbral del Milenio* (50 interviews with prominent Mexicans over the age of 70). He is currently working on *Te doy mi Palabra de Amor II* and *Dichas y Dichos Insólitos de la Gastronomía Mexicana*.

Phrases and Expressions in Spanish

a

a altas horas de la madrugada (adv.) —In the small hours of the morning

a disgusto (adv.) —1) Reluctantly ▪ *Aceptó el papel de Malvolio a disgusto. He accepted the role of Malvolio reluctantly.* —2) Unhappy; not pleased ▪ *Está a disgusto en ese trabajo. He is not at all happy in that job.*

a duras penas (adv.) —Barely ▪ *A duras penas tuve suficiente para el taxi. I barely had enough for the taxi.*

a eso de (x hora) (adv.) —At about (x time) ▪ *Te espero a eso de las cuatro. I'll expect you around four.*

a estas alturas (adv.) —At this point of the game ▪ *¿Cómo me dejas solo a estas alturas? How can you walk out on me at this point of the game? (in these circumstances)*

a fin de cuentas (adv.) —In the end; when you come right down to it (*lit.* once the calculations are done) ▪ *A fin de cuentas no presentaron el proyecto. In the end, they didn't submit the project.*

a fines de …; a finales de … (adv.) —At the end of …; late in the month (week, etc.); in late … ▪ *Volveré a fines de junio. I'll be back in late June.*

a fondo (adv.) —1) In-depth ▪ *Se necesita un estudio más a fondo para determinar el verdadero valor de esta antigüedad. A more in-depth study is necessary to determine the true value of this antique.* —2) Thoroughly ▪ *Le prometí a mi jefe que investigaría a fondo este faltante de dinero. I promised my boss that I would investigate the problem of the missing money thoroughly.*

a juro (adv.) —*(Ven)* (slang) A must ▪ *Tienes que terminar ese trabajo a juro. You've got to finish the work, no matter what.*

a la fresca viruta (adv.) —*(Arg)* (slang) Carelessly; without thinking or planning ▪ *Luis hace todo a la fresca viruta. Luis does everything kind of half-assed…*

a la hora de la hora (adv.) —When the going gets tough ▪ *No prometas nada. A la hora de la hora, siempre te echas para atrás. Don't promise anything. When the going gets tough, you always back down.*

a la hora de la verdad (adv.) —When the time comes ▪ *No te rajes a la hora de la verdad. Don't turn tail and run when the going gets tough.*

a la larga (adv.) —Eventually; in the long run ▪ *Está bonito el cachorro, pero a la larga va a ser una lata. The puppy is sweet, but in the long run,* *it'll be a nuisance.*

a las mil maravillas (adv.) —Wonderfully well ▪ *Raúl tocó la guitarra a las mil maravillas. Raul played the guitar extremely well.*

a las mil y quinientas (adv.) —In the wee hours of the morning; very late

a lo bestia (adv.) —(slang) Excessively; in a rough and uncivilized way ▪ *Estoy trabajando a lo bestia. I'm working like a dog.*

a lo idiota (adv.) —(vulgar) In a not very bright way ▪ *Estás jugando a lo idiota. ¿Qué te pasa? You are playing very stupidly. What's wrong with you?*

a lo mejor (adv.) —Perhaps; maybe; could be; possibly ▪ *A lo mejor no viene Jorge. Jorge may not come.*

a lo tarugo (adv.) —*(Mex)* (slang) In a not very bright way

a lo tonto (adv.) —In a not very bright way

a más no poder (adv.) —With all one's might and main ▪ *Adelantamos el trabajo a más no poder. We got as far with the work as it was humanly possible.*

a más tardar (adv.) —At the latest; no later than ▪ *El coche tiene que estar listo a más tardar a las cuatro, porque a esa hora nos vamos. The car has to be ready no later than four o'clock, because that's when we're leaving.*

a mediados de … (adv.) —In the middle of …; in mid-… ▪ *Llegamos a México a mediados de abril. We arrive in Mexico in mid-April.*

a morir (adv.) —Until (something) dies, runs out, peters out, comes to an end, etc. ▪ *El partido de esta noche es a morir. Tonight's game is to the death.*

¡A otro perro con ese hueso! —Bullshit!; I really don't believe you!

a pasos agigantados (adv.) —By leaps and bounds ▪ *Sandra está mejorando en el tenis a pasos agigantados. Sandra's tennis is improving by leaps and bounds.*

a pedir de boca (adv.) —Just perfect ▪ *Yo tenía mis dudas acerca de ese conjunto musical, pero la fiesta salió a pedir de boca. I had my doubts about that musical group, but the party worked out beautifully.*

¡A poco! —*(Mex)* Really?; no kidding!; seriously?

¿A poco no? —*(Mex)* Don't you agree?; Am I right? ▪ *Está bonito. ¿A poco no? Pretty, don't you think?*

a principios de (adv.) —At the beginning of; in early

a propósito (adv.) —1) Incidentally; by the way ▪ *¡Mira qué bonitos perros! A propósito, ¿cómo está la perrita que te regalaron?* Look what lovely dogs! By the way, how's the little dog you got as a gift? —2) On purpose ▪ *¡No te hagas! Hiciste eso a propósito.* Don't pretend! You did that on purpose.

a puros ... (golpes, gritos, etc.) (adv.) —*(Mex)* Only when you hit (whack) him; only if you yell at him ▪ *Entiende a puros gritos.* She only understands things when you yell at her.

¡A que no! —Want to bet? (neg.)

¡A que sí! —Want to bet? (aff.)

a regañadientes (adv.) —Reluctantly; grudgingly ▪ *A regañadientes aceptó pagar.* He paid up very grudgingly.

¡A saber! —*(ES)* Who knows!

a secas (adv.) —*(Mex)* Without any trimmings or extras ▪ *Nada de Señor licenciado, llámame Pedro, a secas.* Forget the title. Just call me Pedro, plain and simple.

a toda costa (adv.) —At whatever cost; no matter what, how, when, etc. ▪ *Voy a lograr mi propósito a toda costa.* I'm going to achieve my goal no matter what.

a todo dar (adj.) —*(Mex)* Great!; terrific!

¡A todo meter! (adj.) —*(Mex)* (slang) Great!; terrific!; cool!; wonderful!

a ver si pega (adv.) —*(Mex)* To see if it works; to see if some strategy, scheme or plan works (*lit.* to see if it sticks) ▪ *Voy a pedirle prestado, a ver si pega.* I'm going to hit him for a loan... see if it works.

aborregar(se) (v.) —*(Peru)* (slang) To become intimidated ▪ *Cuando vio el puente colgante, se aborregó.* When he saw the suspension bridge, he looked really intimidated.

¡Abrete!; ¡Abrase! (v.) —*(Col)* (slang) Leave! Beat it!

abrir(se) (v.) —*(Col)* To leave; to scram; to beat it; to take off

abrir(se) de capa (v.) —To speak frankly and sincerely (*lit.* to open your cape) ▪ *A mí no me dijo nada, pero supe que se abrió de capa con Alonso.* He didn't say anything to me, but I hear he really opened up with Alonso.

aburrir(se) como ostra (v.) —To be bored to tears (*lit.* to be as bored as an oyster)

¡Abusado(a)! (adj.) —*(Mex)* (slang) Careful!; Use your head!; Stay on your toes!

---

acabar por (v.) —To end up doing (X) ▪ *Acabaron por irse. They ended up leaving.*

acariñar a (alguien) (v.) —*(Peru)* (slang) To caress

acelerado(a) (adj.) (adv.) —Aggressive; excited

acelerar(se) (v.) —To get uptight, annoyed, carried away, angry, etc. ▪ *Está bien, voy a regresar el vestido a la tienda. ¡No te aceleres! OK, I'll send the dress back to the store. Don't get carried away!*

acochinar (v.) —*(Col)* (slang) To frighten (from **cochino**: pig)

acordeón (n.) —*(Mex)* A crib sheet (used to cheat on a test or examination)

actuar como si nada (v.) —To play it cool ▪ *Si el gerente te pregunta algo acerca del pleito, actúa como si nada. If the manager asks anything about the fight, just play it cool.*

acurrucar(se) (v.) —To curl up in a comfortable, cozy position on a bed, sofa, etc., or in someone's arms ▪ *La niña estaba acurrucada en el sofá junto a la chimenea, con el gato acurrucado en sus brazos. The little girl was curled up on the sofa next to the fireplace, with the cat curled up in her arms.*

achanchado(a) (n.) (adj.) —*(Peru)* (slang) An inhibited person; a car that doesn't run well

achanchar(se) (v.) —*(Peru)* (slang) To become inhibited, weakened

achicopalar(se) (v.) —*(Mex)* (slang) To become very sad, frightened and discouraged ▪ *Desde que perdió a su novia, está muy achicopalado. Since he lost his girlfriend, he has been really down in the dumps.*

achicharrar(se) (v.) —*(Mex)* To burn (something); to get burned; to feel very hot ▪ *Me estoy achicharrando. I'm dying of the heat! ¡Ya achicharraste la tortilla! You've burned the tortilla!*

achichinque (achichincle or **achichintle)** (n.) —*(Mex)* Helper (derogatory) ▪ *No trajiste a tu achichinque. You didn't bring your assistant.*

¡Adió! —*(Mex)* Used as an interjection to express incredulity or doubt ▪ *¿Qué? ¿Ya son las seis? ¡Adió! What? It's six o'clock already? You're kidding?!*

¡Adiosito! (n.) —Bye-bye; diminutive of **adiós** (expresses a fond goodbye prior to a brief absence)

afanar(se) (v.) —1) To work hard on (something) ▪ *Nos afanamos en terminar a tiempo el vestido para la boda. We really worked very hard to get the dress ready in time for the wedding.* —2) (underworld jargon) To steal

afilar (v.) —*(Arg)* (slang) To chat with your sweetheart

aflatar(se) (v.) —*(Gua)* (slang) To be afraid, scared

aflojar(sele) el ruedo (v.) —*(CR)* (slang) To get really scared (*lit.* to lose control of my lower sphincter) ▪ *Se me aflojó el ruedo.* *I was so scared, I nearly dirtied my pants!*

agandallado(a) (adj.) —*(Mex)* (youth) Not a pal; not friendly ▪ *Pancho anda muy agandallado últimamente.* *Pancho has been a downright jerk recently.*

agandalle (n.) —*(Mex)* (youth) Unfriendly act

agarrar con las manos en la masa a (alguien) (v.) —To catch (someone) red-handed ▪ *A Luis lo agarraron con las manos en la masa.* *Luis was caught red-handed.*

agarrar de botana a (alguien) (v.) —(slang) To make fun of (someone) ▪ *Es el tipo de persona a quien todo mundo agarra de botana.* *He's the type of guy that everyone makes fun of.*

agarrar(se) del chongo (v.) —(slang) To brawl; to fight (applied to women) (*lit.* to grab each other by the bun of hair) ▪ *En una reunión muy elegante, la amante y la esposa de Rodolfo se agarraron del chongo.* *At a very posh event, Luis's mistress and his wife had a knockdown, drag-out fight.*

agarrar en curva a (alguien) (v.) —To catch (someone) off guard ▪ *Adelina me agarró en curva cuando me propuso hacer ese negocio.* *Adelina caught me off guard when she suggested we go into business together.*

agarrar la onda (v.) —(youth) To get in the groove; to get the picture; to get with it ▪ *No entiendes nada. ¡Agarra la onda!* *You don't understand anything! Get on the ball!!*

agarrar su patín (v.) —(slang) To start and/or keep doing (something) that other people find hard to stop (*lit.* to grab your skate) ▪ *Agarró su patín contando chistes y no hubo quien lo callara.* *He got carried away telling jokes and there was no shutting him up.*

agarrar vuelo (v.) —To work up speed or intensity

aguacero (n.) —*(Ven)* (slang) A downpour; a lot; a whole bunch ▪ *Tengo un aguacero de problemas.* *I have a heap of problems.*

aguantar carros y carretas (v.) —To have the capacity to take a lot of negative acts or nonsense from (someone)

¡Aguas! —*(Mex)* (slang) Watch out!; careful! (used as a warning of imminent danger)

agüitar(se) (v.) —To become disheartened

¡Ahí la llevas! —*(Mex)* (slang) Way to go! (sarcastic) ▪ *Nada más quemaste* *seis salchichas. ¡Ahí la llevas! You only burned six sausages. Way to go!*

¡Ahí muere! —*(Mex)* (slang) Call it quits!; That's enough!

¡Ahí te voy! —(slang) Watch out!; Here I come!

ahora mismo; ahorita (adv.) —Right now

ahoritita (adv.) —In this very moment; right this instant

al abrigo de (adv.) —In the protection/shelter of ... ▪ *Corrieron a ponerse al abrigo del techo. They ran under the roof to get out of the rain.*

al ahí se va (adv.) —*(Mex)* Carelessly; without thinking or planning ▪ *Luis hace todo al ahí se va. Luis does everything kind of half-assed...*

al aventón (adv.) —Carelessly; without thinking or planning ▪ *Luis hace todo al aventón. Luis does everything kind of half-assed...*

al chas chas (adv.) —*(Mex)* (slang) In cash; cash on the line (non-slang: en efectivo) ▪ *En este restaurante no aceptan tarjetas de crédito. Hay que pagar al chas chas. They don't accept credit cards at this restaurant. Payment is strictly cash on the line.*

al chilazo (adv.) —*(Mex)* (slang) Carelessly; without thinking or planning ▪ *Luis hace todo al chilazo. Luis does everything kind of half-assed...*

al fin y al cabo (adv.) —After all; anyway ▪ *Al fin y al cabo no perdimos tanto. We didn't lose so much after all. Nos quedamos a ver la TV, al fin y al cabo hacía mucho frío para salir. We stayed home and watched TV. It was too cold to go out, anyway.*

al hilo (adv.) —One after the other ▪ *Ganó ocho juegos al hilo. He won eight games in a row.*

al otro día (adv.) —The next day ▪ *Al otro día había mejorado. He was better the next day.*

al parecer (adv.) —Apparently; supposedly ▪ *Nadie esperaba su muerte. Al parecer, era diabética. No one expected her death. Apparently, she was a diabetic.*

al tanteo (adv.) —*(Mex)* Haphazardly; by guesswork; said of (something) that is done without really knowing what is being done ▪ *¿Sabes algo, o lo dices al tanteo? Do you know something for a fact, or are you just blabbing?*

alebrestar(se) (v.) —To get all riled up

alentar(se) (v.) —*(Hon, Ven)* (slang) To get over an illness; to get better after being sick

aletazo (n.) —*(Hon)* (slang) Fraud

algo es algo —It's better than nothing (*lit.* something is something)

alivianar(se) (v.) —1) To cheer up ▪ *Hay que alivianarnos. Nada ganamos con estar deprimidos a causa de este problema.* We really have to cheer up. We gain nothing by being glum about this. —2) To get high (any drug) ▪ *¿Quieres alivianarte con nosotros? Cierra la puerta.* Do you want to get high with us? Close the door.

aliviar(se) (v.) —*(Mex)* To give birth ▪ *¿Te vas a aliviar en esa maternidad?* You're going to have the baby at that clinic?

alma de Dios (n.) —A lovely person; a dear (kind, generous, sympathetic, etc.) person (*lit.* a soul of God) ▪ *Pablo es un alma de Dios. No pudo haber echado este perro a la calle.* Pablo couldn't have thrown this dog out in the street. He's a dear.

alucinar a (alguien) (v.) —*(Mex)* To be fed up with (someone)'s constant and not very welcome presence ▪ *Ya alucino a tu hermano. Lo veo hasta en la sopa.* I'm rather sick of your brother's constant presence. I see him everywhere I turn.

amapuchar(se) (v.) —*(Ven)* (slang) To kiss/make out heavily

amolar(la) (v.) —*(Mex)* (slang) To do (something) crummy; to spoil things ▪ *¡Mira nada más lo que le hiciste a mi camisa! ¡Ya la amolaste, tarugo!* Just look what you did to my shirt! You screwed things up, stupid!

amuchar (v.) —*(Bol)* (slang) To increase (from **mucho**: much)

amuinado(a) (adj.) —*(Mex)* Angry; sad; down in the dumps (**amohinar**: a corruption of **estar mohino**: to anger or sadden)

andar a la cuarta pregunta (v.) —To be totally broke

andar amolado(a) (v.) —*(Mex)* (slang) To be in a bad way (as concerns money or health) ▪ *Me encantaría acompañarlos a Cancún, pero no puedo. Ando muy amolado de dinero.* I'd love to go with you all to Cancún, but I can't. I'm really broke.

andar(se) con rodeos (v.) —To beat around the bush ▪ *Ve al grano. No te andes con rodeos.* Get to the point. Stop beating around the bush.

andar chueco(a) (v.) —*(Mex)* (slang) To be crooked (usually as concerns the authorities, especially the tax authorities)

andar de boca en boca (v.) —To be on everyone's lips; to be the talk of the town (*lit.* to go from mouth to mouth)

andar de capa caída (v.) —To be depressed, downhearted (*lit.* to go around with your cape drooping) ▪ *Edgar anda de capa caída porque no lo ascendieron como esperaba.* Edgar is all downhearted because he wasn't promoted as he expected.

andar de la ceca a la meca (v.) —To go to many places ▪ *Para encontrar el regalo tuvimos que andar de la ceca a la meca. We had to go to a million places to find just the right gift.*

andar de malas (v.) —1) To be in a period of bad luck ▪ *Le volvieron a robar el coche. De veras que anda de malas. His car was stolen again. He really is having a streak of bad luck.* —2) To be in a bad mood ▪ *Lleva dos horas encerrado en su cuarto. Anda de malas. He's been locked up in his room for two hours. He's in a bad mood.*

andar de picos pardos (v.) —(slang) To sow your wild oats

andar de pinta (v.) —*(Uru)* To be all dolled up; to be in your Sunday best ▪ *Anda de pinta porque va a la boda de su amiga. She's all dolled up because she's going to her friend's wedding.*

andar en bola (v.) —*(Arg)* (slang) To be naked

andar en fachas (v.) —To be dressed in dreadful old rags; to look awful (as concerns clothes) (*lit.* to go around in sloppy clothes)

andar en la baba (v.) —(slang) To be off on a cloud; to be daydreaming (*lit.* to be drooling) ▪ *Ya volviste a tirar el café. Andas en la baba. You've spilled the coffee again. You really are off on a cloud.*

andar en las nubes (v.) —1) To be on cloud nine (*lit.* to be in the clouds) —2) To be (mentally) somewhere else (daydreaming)

andar erizo(a) (v.) —(youth) To be in need of a drug; to need a fix ▪ *Ese chavo anda bien erizo. That kid needs a fix.*

andar hasta la madre (v.) —(vulgar) To be blind drunk

andar norteado(a) (v.) —To be disoriented ▪ *No conozco la ciudad y ando norteado. I don't know the city and I've lost my bearings.*

andar(se) por las ramas (v.) —To beat around the bush ▪ *Ve al grano. No te andes por las ramas. Get to the point. Stop beating around the bush.*

andar volado(a) (v.) —(slang) To be very keen; to be infatuated with (someone) who is not likely to pay much attention to you

antojitos (n.) —*(Mex)* Finger food, usually eaten at sidewalk stands without even sitting down

apachar (v.) —*(Gua)* (slang) To push ▪ *¡Apáchalo para allá! Push it over there!*

apantallar(se) (v.) —(slang) To allow yourself to be impressed; to allow (someone) to put one over on you

apantallar a (alguien) (v.) —(slang) To impress (someone)

apapachar (v.) —To caress and/or embrace fondly and affectionately; to fondle ▪ *¿Por qué siempre tienes que estar apapachando a ese gato rascuache?* Why do you always have to be fondling that ratty cat? *A la abuela le encanta apapachar a sus nietos.* Grandmother loves to hug and squeeze her grandchildren.

aparentar edad (años) (v.) —To appear to be a certain age ▪ *Aparenta menos edad (años) de la (de los) que tiene.* He looks younger than he actually is.

apenas a tiempo (adv.) —In the nick of time ▪ *Llegaste apenas a tiempo. Ya me iba.* You're here just in the nick of time. I was just leaving.

aplatanado(a) (adj.) —*(Mex)* (youth) Slow; listless; lacking energy (lit. feeling like a squishy, overripe banana) ▪ *Ya sé por qué Lalo anda tan aplatanado. Tiene la presión baja.* Now I know why Lalo isn't his usual, peppy self. His blood pressure is low.

aplatanar(se) (v.) —*(Mex)* (slang) To become listless and dispirited

apoquinar (v.) —*(Mex)* (slang) To pay up; to hand over the dough; to fork it over ▪ *No me salgas con tus excusas de siempre. ¡Tienes que apoquinar!* Don't hand me your usual excuses. You've got to fork it over!

apretar (v.) —To increase in strength, degree, speed, etc. ▪ *Apretó la lluvia.* The rain intensified. *Apretó el frío.* It got colder. *Apretó el paso.* He started walking faster.

aprovechado(a) (n.) (adj.) —A person who takes advantage of (someone or something); a person who will stop at very little to seize an opportunity to benefit himself

¡Apúrate! (¡Apúrese!) —Step on it!

aquél (aquella) (pron.) —Pronoun used when you want to avoid mentioning the name of a person (e.g. you-know-who) ▪ *¿Qué pasó con aquél?* What happened with you-know-who?

aquello (pron.) —Pronoun for things, used when you want to avoid mentioning a particular thing (e.g. you-know-what) ▪ *Aquello no ha llegado.* The you-know-what hasn't arrived.

argüende (n.) —*(Mex)* (slang) Noisy, gossipy chatter ▪ *A Lupe le encanta el argüende. ¿No crees?* Lupe just loves to be in the thick of the fray (any argument), doesn't she?

armar(se) la gorda (v.) —*(Mex)* (slang) To start a fight ▪ *Si siguen gritándose, se va a armar la gorda.* If they keep on yelling at each other, there's going to be a fight.

arrumaco (n.) —*(Mex, Arg, Cuba, Chi)* A caress

arrunchar(se) (v.) —To curl up on a bed, sofa, etc. when you're cold and tired

¡Atáscate ahora que hay lodo! —Take advantage of the situation!; *(Mex)* (slang) Go ahead and make a pig of yourself! ▪ *Carlos trajo seis tortas para los dos. ¡Atáscate ahora que hay lodo! Carlos brought six sandwiches just for us two. Dig in!*

atender a cuerpo de rey a (alguien) (v.) —To wait on (someone) hand and foot ▪ *Cuando estuvimos en Perú, los parientes de Carlos nos atendieron a cuerpo de rey. When we were in Peru, Carlos's relatives treated us like royalty.*

aterrizar (v.) —(youth) To come back down to Earth after the effects of marijuana (*lit.* to land)

atorrante (n.) (adj.) —*(Arg)* (slang) A lazy bum

atracador (n.) (adj.) —*(Chi)* (slang) A person who feels up a woman; (someone) whose sexual advances are heavyhanded and unwelcome

atracar (v.) —*(Chi)* (slang) To feel up a woman

atrancar (v.) —*(Mex)* To lock (*lit.* to bolt)

aventón (n.) —A ride (*lit.* a throw) ▪ *¿Me das un aventón? Will you give me a ride?*

avionada (n.) —*(Col)* (slang) The act of taking advantage (usually unfair) of (someone or something)

B

b

babosada (n.) —*(Mex, CA)* (slang) A silly act ▪ *Juan siempre dice puras babosadas. Juan is always saying something silly (fooling around).*

babosear(se) (v.) —*(Cuba)* (slang) To neck heavily; to make out

babosear a (alguien) (v.) —*(Mex)* (slang) To push (someone) around ▪ *¡Ojo! No dejes que te babosee. Don't let him get the better of you. Careful!*

baboso(a) (n.) (adj.) —(slang) A not very bright person

bajar(se) de la mula (v.) —*(Ven)* To bribe ▪ *Para lograr el permiso tuve que bajarme de la mula. The only way to get the permit was to offer a bribe.*

bajar(le) los humos a (alguien) (v.) —To bring (someone) down a few notches ▪ *Creo que voy a tener que bajarle los humos a ese tipo. I think I'm going to have to bring that guy down a few notches.*

bajativo (n.) —*(Chi)* (slang) Liqueur after meals (from **bajar**: to get down) ▪ *Comí mucho, necesito un bajativo. I ate too much. I need something to get it all moving (assist the digestive process).*

bajonear(se) (v.) —(slang) To get nostalgic or homesick ▪ *Lejos de mi novio, me bajoneo. I get blue when I'm far from my boyfriend.*

balín (adj.) —*(Mex)* Fake; counterfeit ▪ *Esta refacción es balín. This spare part is fake.*

¡Barájamela más despacio! (v.) —Run that by me again more slowly (*lit.* to shuffle more slowly) ▪ *Lo siento, pero no entendí nada. Barájamela más despacio. Sorry, but I didn't understand. Run that by me again more slowly.*

baras (adj.) —*(Mex)* (slang) Cheap; inexpensive (from **barato**: cheap) ▪ *Mira, compré bien baras este suéter en el mercado. Look. I got this sweater real cheap at the market.*

barbaridad (n.) —1) A tremendous amount of (something) ▪ *Tengo una barbaridad de trabajo. I have a ton of work.* —2) A dreadful, very daring, wild, crazy or despicable act ▪ *Hizo muchas barbaridades cuando era joven. He did a lot of wild (crazy, daring) things when he was young.*

barbear a (alguien) (v.) —To suck up to (someone); to flatter (someone)

¡Basta! —Enough!

bemba (n.) —*(Cuba)* (slang) Thick lips ▪ *Tú tienes la bemba colorá. You have painted your lips red.* (Words of a Cuban song (rumba))

berenjenal (n.) —*(Ven, Chi, Cuba, Gua)* (slang) Difficulties

berrinche (n.) —1) *(Mex)* A tantrum ▪ *¡Estás muy viejo para hacer*

berrinches! *You're too old to be having tantrums!* —2) *(Ven)* (slang) Urinal smell

billetiza (n.) —*(Mex)* (youth) Money

bocabajear a (alguien) (v.) —To humiliate (someone)

bocas (n.) —*(CR)* Hors d'œuvres

bojote (n.) —*(Col)* (slang) A parcel or package

bola de (algo) (n.) —*(Mex)* A bunch of (something) ▪ *Bola de vagos. A bunch of loiterers.*

bolo (n.) (adj.) —*(Gua)* (slang) Drunk

(un) bonche (n.) —(slang) A lot of something (from bunch) ▪ *Tenemos que lavar un buen bonche de ropa. We have to wash a whole lot of clothes.*

boquiflojo(a) (n.) (adj.) —Gossipy loudmouth

boquitas (n.) —*(Gua)* (slang) Snacks

borlote (n.) —(slang) A big stink ▪ *Hizo un borlote porque le rayaron el coche. He made a big stink because they scratched his car.*

bote (botellón) (n.) —*(Mex)* (slang) Jail; the clink; the cooler; the slammer

brillar por su ausencia (v.) —To be very conspicuously absent (*lit.* to shine by your absence) ▪ *En la junta Carlos brilló por su ausencia. Carlos's absence was glaringly obvious to everyone at the meeting.*

bulla (n.) —*(Gua)* (slang) A party ▪ *La bulla estuvo muy buena. The party was great!*

buque (n.) —*(Chi)* (slang) A large, flashy car

buscabullas (n.) (adj.) —*(Mex)* (slang) A noisy troublemaker

¡Buso(a)! (adj.) —*(Mex)* (slang) Careful!; Use your head!; Stay on your toes!

cabecear (v.) —To doze off in a sitting position

cachaco (n.) —*(Peru)* (slang) Policeman ▪ *La calle estaba llena de cachacos. The street was full of cops.*

cachada (n.) —*(Uru, Arg)* (slang) A practical joke

cachar a (alguien) (v.) —1) *(Mex)* (slang) To catch (someone) doing something —2) *(Arg, Ecu)* To deceive; to ridicule; to make fun of; to jeer

cachar granizo (v.) —*(Mex)* (slang) To be or act gay (men) *(lit.* to catch hail) ▪ *Creo que ese muchacho cacha granizo. I think that boy is gay.*

cachondear(se) (v.) —To neck; to make out ▪ *No quiero que se estén cachondeando en el cine, ¿oyeron? No making out at the movies, you hear?*

cada mil años (adv.) —Once in a blue moon

caer(se) (con la lana) (v.) —*(Mex)* (slang) To pay up; to hand over the dough; to fork it over ▪ *Ya ví que te pagaron. ¡Ahora, cáete (cáete con la lana)! I saw you got paid. Now hand over the dough!*

caer(le) a (alguien) (v.) —To visit (someone); drop in on (someone); to pop in on (someone) ▪ *¿Qué te parece si te caigo mañana en la tarde? Would it be all right if I dropped in tomorrow afternoon?*

caer al (puro) pelo a (alguien) (v.) —*(Mex)* (slang) To suit (someone) to a T; to be just the thing; to be just what one wants or needs ▪ *Tu regalo me cayó al puro pelo. Your gift was just what I needed.*

caer(le) bien (mal) a (alguien) (v.) —To like; When speaking of a dish or a beverage of some kind, this means it is enjoyed (tasty, satisfying). When **mal** is used instead of **bien**, the meaning is the opposite. ▪ *No sé por qué Lucía te cae mal. A mí siempre he ha caído muy bien. I don't know why you don't like Lucía. I've always liked her very much. Me cayó muy bien ese vaso de leche caliente. That glass of warm milk went down very well (made me feel better). No comas el puerco. Sabes que siempre te cae mal. Don't eat the pork. You know it never agrees with you.*

caer(le) como anillo al dedo a (alguien) (v.) —To suit (someone) to a T *(lit.* to fit like a ring on a finger) ▪ *El dinero que me prometió mi abuelo me va a caer como anillo al dedo. The money my grandfather promised me is going to be most welcome.*

caer(se) de la reata (v.) —*(Mex)* To be caught or found out lying

caer(le) de variedad a (alguien) (v.) —(slang) To be amusing ▪ *Tu amigo es muy chistoso, me cae de variedad. Your friend is very amusing. He really makes me laugh.*

---

caer(le) el chahuiztle a (alguien) (v.) —*(Mex)* (slang) To have really bad luck; to have (something) awful happen (like an unpleasant visit) (*lit.* to have your corn suddenly blighted by **chahuiztle**, a deadly plant disease) ▪ *Llegaron mis cuñados para quedarse el fin de semana. ¡Me cayó el chahuiztle! My brothers-in-law have arrived to stay for the weekend! What a bummer!*

caer(le) el veinte a (alguien) (v.) —(slang) To finally realize or understand (something); to catch on (This refers to something not working until the coin drops and makes things go, as for a public telephone.) ▪ *Le eché varias indirectas, pero nunca le cayó el veinte de que era mi cumpleaños. I dropped several hints, but he never caught on that it was my birthday.*

caer en blandito (v.) —To be fortunate enough to have a situation turn out extremely well without much effort (*lit.* to fall on a soft surface) ▪ *Caíste en blandito. ¡Qué bonito trabajar para un tío que te consiente tanto! You're on easy street! Must be great to work for an uncle who pampers you the way this one does!*

caer(le) gordo(a) a (alguien) (v.) —*(Mex)* (slang) To be obnoxious (*lit.* to fall heavily on someone) ▪ *Por favor no invites a tu primo. Me cae muy gordo. Please don't invite your cousin. He's really obnoxious (I really don't like him).*

café corriente (n.) —*(CR)* Black coffee, as opposed to cappuccino or espresso

cahuinero(a) (adj.) —*(Chi)* (slang) A gossipy person ▪ *Ester es una cahuinera. Ester is a gossipy busybody.*

caído(a) de la cama (n.) —*(Uru)* A newborn

caído(a) de la hamaca (n.) —*(Ecu)* A newborn

caído(a) del catre (n.) —*(Arg, Chi)* A newborn

caído(a) del nido (n.) —*(Mex)* A newborn

caído(a) del tapanco (n.) —*(Gua)* A newborn

¡Caifás con la lana!; ¡Cayitos! —*(Mex)* (slang) Pay up!; Hand over the dough!; Fork over the dough!

calentar(le) la cabeza a (alguien) (v.) —To prejudice (someone) against (someone or something) (*lit.* to heat up one's head)

calentar las orejas a (alguien) (v.) —*(Ven)* (slang) To talk up a girl; to make amorous insinuations

calzoneta (n.) —*(ES)* Bathing suit ▪ *No puedo nadar porque se me olvidó la calzoneta. I can't swim because I forgot my bathing suit.*

calzonudo(a) (n.) (adj.) —*(Mex)* (slang) Stubborn ▪ *Se salió con la suya. Es muy calzonudo.* He got away with it. He's really got some nerve!!

camellar (v.) —*(Col, Mex)* (slang) To work hard ▪ *Tuvimos que camellar mucho para terminar a tiempo.* We had to work really hard to finish on time.

caminar por la vereda (v.) —*(Arg)* To walk on the sidewalk

campechano(a) (n.) (adj.) —*(Mex)* (slang) A nice fellow ▪ *Tu primo es muy campechano.* Your cousin is very unpretentious and frank.

canchanchán (n.) —*(Mex)* (slang) Gofer; menial worker on a construction site

cantar la guácara (v.) —*(Mex)* (slang) To throw up

cantar(le) otro gallo (v.) —Things would be different ▪ *Con ese dinero otro gallo me cantaría.* With that money, things would be different!

cantar(le) sus verdades a (alguien) (v.) —To give (someone) a piece of your mind ▪ *No tienes los pantalones para cantarle sus verdades a tu esposa.* You haven't got the guts to give your wife a piece of your mind.

cantinear (v.) —*(Gua)* (slang) To visit the girlfriend

cara de pocos amigos (n.) —A nasty look (*lit.* a face of few friends) ▪ *¿Quién es ése que está allá con cara de pocos amigos?* Who's that over there with the scowl?

carcacha (n.) —Jalopy

cargar con el muerto (v.) —To take the blame for (something) (*lit.* to carry the body) ▪ *Si lo haces, no me involucres a mí. No quiero cargar con el muerto como la última vez.* If you do it, don't get me involved. I have no intention of taking the blame for it, like last time.

cargar(se) el pintor a (alguien) (v.) —1) *(Mex)* To die; i.e. the great painter took him off ▪ *Al mafioso ése se lo cargó el pintor hace una semana.* That thug died a week ago. —2) To be or get fed up ▪ *¡Me carga el pintor! Otra vez viene mi suegra a comer.* Hell's bells! My mother-in-law is coming to lunch again!

cargar(le) la mano a (alguien) (v.) —To give (someone) a hard time ▪ *Le cargas mucho la mano a ese pobre niño. Sólo tiene siete años.* You're too hard on that poor kid. He's only seven years old.

caribear (v.) —*(Ven)* (slang) To take advantage of (someone or something)

caribería (n.) —*(Ven)* (slang) An unfair act ▪ *Le hicieron una caribería.* They pulled a fast one on him.

carne de cañón (n.) —Cannon fodder

carrerear a (alguien) (v.) —To pressure (someone) into doing (something) really fast ▪ *No me carrerees. Si me apuro, me sale mal.* *Don't rush me. If I hurry, I'll spoil it.*

carro (n.) —*(CR, Mex)* Car

casar(se) con hombre en base (v.) —*(Ven)* To get married when you're already pregnant ▪ *Julia se casó con hombre en base.* *Julia was pregnant when she got married.*

caso de fuerza mayor (n.) —Act of God

castigar (v.) —*(Peru, Mex)* To purposely ignore your boyfriend or girl-friend in order to heighten his/her yearning for you

catire (n.) —*(Col)* (slang) A blond; a fair-haired person ▪ *Es raro encontrar un catire por estos rumbos.* *It's unusual to find a fair-haired person around here.*

cervatana (n.) —*(Mex)* (slang) Beer

¡Claro (que no)! —Of course not!

¡Claro (que sí)! —Of course!; Naturally!

clavar (v.) —*(Arg)* (slang) To slap (someone) with (something) ▪ *Me clavaron con una multa.* *They slapped me with a fine.*

clavar(se) (algo) (v.) —*(Mex)* (slang) To steal (something); to pinch (something) ▪ *Se clavó la cartera.* *He stole the wallet.*

clavar el pico (v.) —To fall asleep in a sitting position (from exhaustion) ▪ *Está a punto de clavar el pico, lleva tres noches estudiando sin dormir.* *After three nights of studying and no sleep, he's really falling on his face.*

coco (n.) —(slang) Head (*lit.* coconut)

cócora (n.) —*(Peru)* (slang) Grudge; ill will

cocheche (n.) (adj.) —*(Hon)* (slang) Effeminate

codear(se) con (v.) —To rub shoulders with ▪ *Cuando anduve con Angela, me codeaba con muchas celebridades.* *When I was going out with Angela, I rubbed shoulders with a lot of celebrities.*

coger gorrión (v.) —*(Cuba)* (slang) To get nostalgic or homesick ▪ *Cuando estuve en París, cogí corrión.* *When I was in Paris, I got very homesick.*

coima (n.) —*(Arg, Chi)* (slang) Bribe

colgar(se) de la lámpara (v.) —To hit the ceiling; to make a big fuss; to make a stink (*lit.* to hang from lamp) ▪ *Cuando mi papá vea lo que le pasó al coche, se va a colgar de la lámpara.* *When my dad sees what happened to his car, he's going to climb a wall.*

colgar(se) hasta el molcajete (v.) —*(Mex)* To be (way) overdressed ▪ *Estela se veía ridícula. Se colgó hasta el molcajete.* *Estela looked pretty* *silly. She was way overdressed.*

colgar(se) hasta la mano del metate (v.) —*(Mex)* To be (way) over-dressed

colgar los tenis (v.) —*(Mex)* (slang) To kick the bucket (*lit.* to hang up (or hand in) your tennis shoes) ▪ *Qué bueno que el abuelo ya está mejor. Pensé que iba a colgar los tenis. I'm so glad grandfather is doing better. I thought he was going to kick the bucket.*

colgar(le) un milagrito a (alguien) (v.) —To accuse (someone) of (something) ▪ *A Fernando le colgaron el milagrito de ser el padre de ese bebé. Fernando was accused of being the father of that baby.*

comer(selo) (v.) —*(Uru)* (slang) To be very good at ▪ *Luis se comió el examen. The examination was a piece of cake for Luis.*

comer ansias (v.) —(slang) To be anxious or fidgety (*lit.* to eat anxiety)

comer(se) con los ojos a (alguien) (v.) —To stare longingly at (someone)

comer(se) la torta antes de tiempo (v.) —*(Mex)* To have sex before marriage

¡Cómo! —This means "How…!" but is often used to mean "What…!" (I can hardly believe my ears!)

como alma en pena (adv.) —Like a ghost

como alma que lleva el diablo (adv.) —Like a bat out of hell

como Dios manda (adv.) —Properly; correctly (*lit.* as God dictates) ▪ *Muy poca gente sabe bailar el tango como Dios manda. Very few people know how to dance the tango properly.*

como me la(lo) recetó el doctor (adv.) —*(Mex)* (Someone is) just what the doctor ordered ▪ *Esa muchacha que vino con Elena está como me la recetó el doctor. That girl that came with Elena is just what the doctor ordered (very attractive).*

¡Cómo no! —1) Of course! ▪ *¿Me puedes prestar 100 pesos hasta mañana? ¡Cómo no! Can you lend me 100 pesos until tomorrow? Of course!* —2) Suuuure! ▪ *La gitana me dijo que voy a conocer un hombre apuesto con mucho dinero, que me va a porponer matrimonio. ¡Cómo no! The gypsy told me I'm going to meet a handsome man with lots of money, who is going to propose to me. Suuuuuuuuuure!*

como si fuera poco… —To add insult to injury…

compadrear (v.) —*(Arg)* To boast; to be boastful; to posture ▪ *Edgardo siempre anda compadreando. Edgardo is always posturing and boasting about* *his nonexistent accomplishments.*

con ganas (adv.) —With great effort; with great enthusiasm ▪ *Así no vamos a llegar nunca. ¡Rema con ganas! We'll never get there if you row like that. Put some energy into it!*

con la baba caída (adv.) —Stupidly (*lit.* with drool dripping from your mouth)

con la mano en la cintura (adv.) —With the greatest of ease (*lit.* with your hand on your hip) ▪ *Carlos le gana a Pepe en tenis con la mano en la cintura. Carlos can beat Pepe at tennis with his hands tied behind his back.*

¡Con permisito! —A friendlier version of **¡Con permiso!** Excuse me!

¡Con razón! —No wonder!

con sus mejores galas (adv.) —Dressed to kill ▪ *Es una boda muy importante. Quiero que vengas con tus mejores galas. It's a very important wedding. I want you to come dressed to kill.*

con toda su humanidad (adv.) —With all his or her bulk ▪ *Cuando estábamos jugando, tu prima gordota me cayó encima con toda su humanidad. When we were playing, that fat cousin of yours landed on top of me... All 200 pounds of her.*

con trabajo(s) (adv.) —With great difficulty ▪ *Nunca voy a tener para comprar el traje. Con trabajos junté para la camisa. I'll never have enough to pay for the suit. I was barely able to scrape together enough for the shirt.*

conchudo(a) (n.) (adj.) —(slang) A person with a lot of nerve

conecte (n.) —1) *(Mex)* Drug pusher ▪ *Carlos tiene un conecte muy bueno. Carlos has a great drug dealer.* —2) A friend or connection in the right place

conocer el tejemaneje (v.) —*(Mex)* (slang) To know the ropes ▪ *No quiero ir sola a sacar la licencia de construcción. Necesito que venga conmigo alguien que conozca el tejemaneje. I don't want to go for the building permit all by myself. I need someone to come with me who knows the ropes.*

conseguir una pincha (v.) —*(Cuba)* (slang) To get a good job

consultar(lo) con la almohada (v.) —To sleep on (something)

contra viento y marea (adv.) —Come hell or high water

corotos (n.) —*(Ven)* (slang) Things; thingamajigs; stuff; junk

correr por cuenta de (alguien) (v.) —To be on (someone) ▪ *Estas copas corren por mi cuenta. These drinks are on me.*

(una) corta feria (n.) —*(Mex)* (slang) Some money, usually for a favor done ▪ *El chavo te saca la basura por una corta feria. The kid will take* *out your garbage, if you give him some dough.*

cortado(a) por la misma tijera (v.) —Made from the same cloth (*lit.* cut with the same scissors)

coscolino(a) (n.) (adj.) —(slang) A person of loose morals ▪ *Tu tío es un viejo coscolino. Your uncle chases every woman in sight!*

coscorrón (n.) —*(Ven, Mex)* A swat on the head with a fist

costar (mucho) trabajo (v.) —To be very difficult ▪ *Me cuesta mucho trabajo traducir al inglés. I find it very difficult to translate into English.*

cotorrear (v.) —1) *(Mex)* (slang) To chat ▪ *Estuvimos cotorreando hasta muy tarde. We were up chatting until all hours.* —2) To pull (someone's) leg ▪ *¿Me estás cotorreando? Are you pulling my leg?*

cotorro(a) (n.) (adj.) —*(Mex)* (slang) Witty; funny; amusing

coyote (n.) —*(Mex)* (slang) A person who handles certain troublesome legal procedures at government agencies for third parties and for a fee, by means of kick-backs and/or bribes (*lit.* coyote)

creer en pajaritos preñados (v.) —*(Ven)* (slang) To be credulous (*lit.* to believe in pregnant birds)

creer(se) la divina garza (v.) —To think a lot of yourself; to be conceited (*lit.* to consider yourself the divine stork) ▪ *Teresa se cree la divina garza porque saca puros dieces. Teresa thinks she's the cat's pajamas because she gets straight As.*

creer(se) la gran cosa (v.) —To think a lot of yourself; to be conceited

cruda (n.) —*(Mex)* A hangover

cruzadilla (n.) —*(ES)* Railroad crossing

cuando la rana eche pelos (adv.) —*(Cuba)* When pigs fly (*lit.* when the frog grows hair)

cuate(a) (n.) —*(Mex)* (slang) Friend; pal; guy; dude; buddy

cuatrapear(sele) (v.) —*(Mex)* (slang) To get things all mixed up ▪ *Iba bien con mi discurso, pero luego se me cuatrapearon las palabras y me puse nervioso. I was doing fine with my speech, but then I got the words all mixed up and got nervous.*

(el) cuco (n.) —*(Chi)* (slang) The devil

cuelga (n.) —*(Mex)* (slang) Gift given to (someone) on his/her birthday or saint's day ▪ *Le dieron una bonita cuelga. He got a very nice birthday present.*

cuento chino (n.) —A cock-and-bull story (*lit.* a Chinese story)

cueste lo que cueste (adv.) —Come hell or high water

Ch

chabacano(a) (adj.) —(slang) Clumsy; corny; vulgar

chacotear (v.) —*(Mex)* (slang) To horse around; to fool around

cháchara(s) (n.) —*(Mex)* (slang) Knickknacks; trifles

chafa(s) (adj.) —*(Mex)* (slang) Fake or cheap; poorly made

¡chale! —*(Mex)* How awful!; Yaaakk!

chamaco(a) (n.) —*(Mex)* Child; kid ▪ **Esos chamacos están haciendo mucho ruido.** *Those kids are making a lot of noise.*

chamagoso(a) (adj.) —*(Mex)* (slang) Tacky; dirty; grubby

chamba (n.) —*(Mex)* (slang) Job; employment

chambear (v.) —*(Mex)* To work ▪ **Gerardo está chambeando en la librería.** *Gerardo is working at the bookstore.*

chambón(a) (n.) (adj.) —(slang) A person who rarely gets anything right

chancleta (n.) —*(Peru)* (slang) A newborn baby girl

chancho (n.) —*(CR)* (slang) Pig (real and figurative)

chanchullo (n.) —*(Mex, Cuba)* (slang) A dirty trick; a scam

changarro (n.) —*(Mex)* (slang) A small business (store, shop, etc.)

chango(a) (n.) —*(Mex)* (slang) A derogatory way of referring to someone (*lit.* monkey)

chaparro(a) (n.) (adj.) —1) *(Mex)* Short person —2) Poor (luck) ▪ **¡Ah, qué suerte tan chaparra!** *What bad luck!*

chato(a) (n.) (adj.) —1) *(Mex)* Pug-nosed —2) *(Peru)* Short

chaviza (n.) —*(Mex)* (slang) Young people ▪ **La chaviza tiene su propio lenguaje.** *Kids have their own language.*

chavo(a) (n.) (adj.) —*(Mex)* (slang) Boy; girl

cheles (n.) —*(Cuba)* (slang) Things; thingamajigs; stuff; junk

cheve (n.) —*(Mex)* (slang) Beer

chévere (adj.) —*(Cuba)* (slang) Very good; very elegant ▪ **Me compré un pantalón muy chévere.** *I bought myself a great pair of pants.*

chicanero(a) (n.) —1) *(Col)* (slang) A boastful loudmouth —2) *(Mex)* A shyster lawyer

chido(a) (adj.) —*(Mex)* (slang) Cool; great; terrific; wonderful ▪ **Tu casa está bien chida.** *Your house is real cool.*

chilango(a) (n.) (adj.)—*(Mex)* (slang) A derogatory way of referring to natives of Mexico City. Mainly used by people from other places in Mexico.

chilpayate (n.) —*(Mex)* Boy

chiluca (n.) —*(Mex)* (slang) Head (*lit.* the name of a hard stone)

chimba (n.) —*(Col)* (slang) (Something) wonderful, great

chimiscolero(a) (n.) (adj.) —*(Mex)* (slang) Busybody; gossip

chimistretas (n.) —*(Mex)* (slang) Things; thingamajigs; stuff; junk

china (n.) —*(Arg, Bol)* (slang) Girl ▪ *¡Eres una china muy linda! You're a lovely girl.*

chinchorrazo (n.) —*(Ven)* (slang) A drink ▪ *Voy a echarme un chinchorrazo. I'm going to have a drink.*

chingana (n.) —*(Peru)* (slang) Bar

chingolingos (n.) —*(Gua)* (slang) Things; thingamajigs; stuff; junk

chínguere (n.) —*(Mex)* (vulgar) A shot of liquor that hits hard, although it can also mean a strong mixed drink, even a long one

chipocludo(a) (n.) (adj.) —1) *(Mex)* (slang) An important person; a VIP ▪ *El gerente es muy chipocludo. The manager is a real VIP.* —2) (Someone or something) that is nice, good, terrific

chiquear (v.) —*(Mex)* (slang) To spoil (someone) ▪ *Ya no chiquees tanto a ese niño. Está insoportable. Stop spoiling that kid. He's unbearable!*

chirimoya (n.) —*(Mex)* (slang) Head

chirinola (n.) —*(Col)* A struggle

(un) chirris (n.) (adj.) —*(Mex)* (slang) Little; small; tiny; a little ▪ *Me falta un chirris para llenar la cubeta. I need just a bit more to fill the bucket.*

chistes (cuentos) colorados (n.) —*(Mex)* Dirty jokes

chiva(s) (n.) —*(Mex)* (slang) Things; thingamajigs; stuff; junk ▪ *¿Qué vas a hacer con todas esas chivas? What are you going to do with all that stuff?*

chivear(se) (v.) —1) *(Mex)* (slang) To be overcome by shyness or embarrassment ▪ *Le pedí que cantara, pero se chiveó. I asked him to sing but he was overcome by shyness.* —2) To go back on your word ▪ *Ofreció ayudar, pero luego se chiveó. She offered to help, but then she went back on her word.*

¡Chócalas! (¡Chócala!) —*(Mex)* Shake hands!; Give me five! (to seal an agreement, a bet, etc.)

chocante (n.) (adj.) —Obnoxious; irritating; unpleasant ▪ *Su cuñado es muy chocante. His brother-in-law is a pain.*

chochear (v.) —*(Ven, Mex)* To act senile ▪ *Mamá pierde todo lo que trae en las manos, ya está chocheando.* Mother loses everything she gets her hands on. She's getting a bit soft in the head.

chochera (n.) —*(Ven, Mex)* A senile act

chocho(a) (n.) (adj.) —*(Ven, Mex)* Old (for people)

cholo(a) (n.) (adj.) —*(Peru, Bol, Ecu)* (slang) Mestizo

cholololo picantero (n.) —*(Peru)* (slang) A person frying fast food for passersby at a street stand

chompa (n.) —*(Peru)* (slang) Sweater ▪ *Juan lleva puesta una chompa nueva.* Juan is wearing a new sweater.

choncho(a) (adj.) —Big; roly-poly; well-filled out; thick ▪ *El niño está muy choncho.* That kid is good and plump.

chones (n.) —*(Mex)* (slang) Panties; also men's shorts or jockey underwear

chorcha (n.) —*(Mex)* (slang) An informal gathering where everyone is talking a mile a minute; a chat

choreto(a) (n.) (adj.) —Bowlegged ▪ *Tiene las piernas choretas.* He is bowlegged.

chorreado(a) (n.) (adj.) —*(Mex)* Dirty; sticky; gummy

(un) chorro (n.) —*(Mex)* (slang) A lot ▪ *Esa chava me gusta un chorro.* I like that girl a whole lot. *Tengo un chorro de trabajo.* I have a lot of work.

choya (n.) —*(Mex)* (slang) Head

chucherías (n.) —*(Mex)* Things; knickknacks; trifles

(una) chulada (n.) —*(Mex)* (slang) Lovely or great ▪ *Ese vestido es una chulada.* That dress is simply gorgeous!

chuleta (n.) —*(Ven)* (slang) A crib sheet; secret notes to copy from in a test

chulo(a) (adj.) —*(Mex)* (slang) Lovely; pretty

chunches (n.) —(slang) Things; thingamajigs; stuff; junk

chupar (v.) —*(Mex)* (slang) To drink (alcohol) (*lit.* to suck)

chupar(se) (v.) —1) *(Chi)* (slang) To give up; to surrender —2) *(Mex)* To lose weight involuntarily

chupar(se) el dedo (v.) —*(Mex)* To be born yesterday (*lit.* to suck your thumb) ▪ *Esos tipos no me van a engañar; no me chupo el dedo.* Those guys aren't going to put one over on me! I wasn't born yesterday.

(el) chupe (n.) —*(Mex)* (slang) The act of drinking alcohol; the act of boozing ▪ *Esos chavos andan en el chupe.* Those kids are out drinking.

churro(a) (n.) —1) *(Col, Uru)* (slang) A handsome or good-looking person (both sexes) —2) A sweet bread made by extruding the batter in a cylindrical shape, then deep-frying in oil and rolling in sugar

ch

chusco —1) (adj.) *(Mex, Peru)* Funny —2) (n.) *(Peru)* (slang) A street dog

(la) chusma (n.) —*(Mex)* A collective noun used to refer to uneducated (loud, coarse, or crass) people as a whole ▪ *A esos juegos de futbol va toda la chusma. Those football games are packed with riffraff.*

¡Dame pelota! —*(CR, Arg)* (slang) Pay attention!

Dando y dando, pajarito volando. —Tit for tat

dar a luz (v.) —To give birth (*lit.* to bring (a baby) out into the light)

dar(le) al clavo (v.) —To hit the nail on the head ▪ *Yo no sabía qué regalarle a Paola en su cumpleaños, pero Arturo le dio al clavo. I had no idea what to give Paola for her birthday, but Arturo hit the nail on the head.*

dar ánimo(s) (v.) —1) To give moral support or courage —2) To encourage. In the negative, **darme ánimos** is a sarcastic way of saying "I really appreciate your support."

dar(le) atole con el dedo a (alguien) (v.) —*(Mex)* To take advantage of (someone's) innocence (*lit.* to feed someone gruel with your finger) ▪ *Hace meses que prometieron aumentarnos el sueldo. Nomás nos están dando atole con el dedo. They promised us raises months ago. They're just stringing us along!*

dar(le) batería a (alguien) (v.) —1) (slang) To give (something) a good go; to put up a fight —2) To satisfy (someone) sexually

dar(se) bomba (v.) —*(Ven)* (slang) To boast; to blow your own horn

dar carpetazo a (algo) (v.) —To hush (something) up

dar(le) coba a (alguien) (v.) —To butter up (someone) ▪ *Esos dos no tienen vergüenza. Siempre están dándole coba a la maestra. Those two have no shame. They are always sucking up to the teacher.*

dar color (v.) —1) *(Mex)* (slang) To take sides; to be clear —2) To pay for (something)

dar(se) color (v.) —(slang) To realize (that …)

dar(le) con la puerta en las narices a (alguien) (v.) —To slam the door in (someone's) face (literally or figuratively)

dar(le) cosa a (alguien) (v.) —*(Mex)* (slang) To get the heebee-jeebies ▪ *Me da cosa tocar las culebras, aunque no hagan nada. It gives me the creeps to touch snakes, even if they are harmless.*

dar(se) cuenta de (de que …) (v.) —1) To realize (that …) —2) To notice (that …) ▪ *No me di cuenta del error. I didn't notice the mistake.*

dar(le) cuerda a (alguien) (v.) —To egg (someone) on; to encourage (someone); to humor (*lit.* to wind someone up) ▪ *Si tu hermano se pone a contar chistes colorados, no le des cuerda. If your brother starts telling dirty jokes, don't egg him on (don't encourage him).*

dar(se) cuerda solo (v.) —To work yourself up; to get carried away (*lit.* to wind yourself up) ▪ *¡Tienes que olvidarla! No sigas dándote cuerda solo. You've got to forget all about her! Stop working yourself up.*

dar(le) cus cus a (alguien) (v.) —1) *(Mex)* (slang) To give (someone) the creeps ▪ *No me gusta dormir con la luz apagada. Me da cus cus. I don't like to sleep with the lights out. It gives me the willies.* —2) To be afraid to do (something)

dar(selas) de (v.) —To pretend to be something you are not; to play the (anything) ▪ *Oscar se las da de contador, pero la verdad es que todavía no se recibe. Oscar passes himself off as an accountant, but the truth is he hasn't got his degree yet.*

dar de alta (v.) —To register; to sign up; to put on the payroll, etc. (except in a hospital, where **dar de alta** is to discharge a patient)

dar de baja (v.) —To take off the registry, list, payroll, etc.

dar (algo) de botana (v.) —(slang) To put out (something) for people to munch on ▪ *Nos dieron unas pizzas miniatura de botana. They put out miniature pizzas for us to munch on with our drinks.*

dar de comer a (alguien) (v.) —To feed (someone or an animal)

dar(le) duro y tupido (v.) —To do (something) with all you've got ▪ *Voy a darle duro y tupido a este trabajo. I'm going to put my all into this work.*

dar el ancho (v.) —To fill the bill ▪ *El muchacho que me recomendaste no da el ancho. The guy you sent me doesn't fill the bill (doesn't qualify).*

dar(le) el avión a (alguien) (v.) —*(Mex)* (slang) To say yes or agree, without really meaning it or without paying attention ▪ *Estuvo de acuerdo con todo lo que le dije. Pero creo que me dio el avión. He agreed with everything I said. But I think he wasn't really listening.*

dar(se) el lujo de (+ verb) (v.) —To be able to afford to (+ verb) (not always connected with money) (*lit.* to give yourself the luxury of (+ verb)) ▪ *En este momento no me puedo dar el lujo de pelearme con él. I can't afford to get him upset right now. Ahora Laura puede darse el lujo de ir a Europa dos veces al año. Now Laura can afford to go off to Europe twice a year.*

dar el magueyazo (v.) —*(Mex)* (slang) To fall over drunk ▪ *Me dio mucha pena cuando dio el magueyazo frente a todos los invitados. It was really embarrassing when he went down like a sack of potatoes in front of all the guests.*

dar(le) el patatús a (alguien) (v.) —*(Ven, Mex)* To have a fit ▪ *¡Pobre*

Laura! *Le dio el patatús porque su hija se casa con ese patán.* Poor Laura! *She had a fit because her daughter is marrying that jerk.*

dar el pitazo (v.) —*(Ven, Mex)* (slang) To blow the whistle on (something)

dar el ranazo (v.) —*(Mex)* (slang) To fall heavily (*lit.* to fall like a frog or bellyflop)

dar(le) el soponcio a (alguien) (v.) —To have a fit

dar el viejazo (v.) —To suddenly become or look old; to lose your youthful looks ▪ *¿Viste a Lola? Ya está dando el viejazo.* Did you see Lola? Age is really catching up with her.

dar en el clavo (v.) —To hit the nail on the head

dar(le) en la torre a (alguien) (v.) —(slang) To do (something) terrible to (someone) (*lit.* to hit someone on the tower)

dar(le) en qué pensar a (alguien) (v.) —To give (someone) food for thought ▪ *Lo que hizo Cecilia de veras que me da en qué pensar.* What Cecilia did really gives me food for thought.

dar(le) entrada a (alguien) (v.) —(slang) To flirt; to invite advances

dar(le) ganas de algo a (alguien) (v.) —To feel like doing something; to be appealing ▪ *No me dan ganas de volver.* I don't feel like going back.

dar(le) gato por liebre a (alguien) (v.) —To gyp or deceive (someone), especially when referring to a purchaser at the market (*lit.* to give the buyer a cat instead of a hare)

dar(se) golpes de pecho (v.) —To appear to be fervently religious (usually feigned) (*lit.* to beat or thump your breast)

dar(le) igual a (alguien) (v.) —Not to care ▪ *No importa si lo llevas hoy o mañana. Me da igual.* It doesn't matter if you take it today or tomorrow. I don't care.

dar(se) ínfulas (v.) —To put on airs ▪ *Desde que se casó con el jefe, Carmen se está dando ínfulas.* Carmen has really been putting on airs since she married the boss.

dar jalón (v.) —(slang) To flirt; to invite advances

dar la casualidad de que ... (v.) —It just so happens that ... ▪ *Da la casualidad de que mi papá es senador.* It just so happens that my father is a senator.

dar lástima (v.) —To be in such a bad way that people feel sorry for you ▪ *Jaime anda tan andrajoso, que da lástima.* Jaime goes around in such dreadful rags that people feel sorry for him.

dar(le) (mucha) lata a (alguien) (v.) —To be a nuisance; to be bugging (someone) all the time; to be a pain ▪ *¿Otra vez quieres que te preste la impresora? ¡Qué lata das! (¡Das mucha lata!)* You want me to lend you the printer again? You sure are a nuisance!

dar(le) madruguete a (alguien) (v.) —(slang) To catch (someone) off guard

dar(le) mala espina a (alguien) (v.) —To give (someone) a nasty feeling; to make (someone) suspicious (*lit.* to give a bad thorn) ▪ *Su tardanza me da mala espina.* He's late, and that makes me nervous.

dar(le) mastuerzo a (alguien) (v.) —(Mex) (slang) To kill; to finish off; to bump off (someone)

dar(le) matarile a (alguien) (v.) —(Mex) (slang) To kill; to finish off; to bump off (someone)

dar(le) ñáñaras a (alguien) (v.) —(Ven, Mex) (slang) To give (someone) the creeps or the heebie-jeebies

dar papaya (v.) —(Col) (slang) To give yourself away

dar(se) paquete (v.) —To be conceited or snotty

dar patadas de ahogado (v.) —To fight a losing battle (*lit.* to thrash around uselessly when you'll drown anyway)

dar(le) pena a (alguien) (v.) —1) To be in such a bad way that people feel sorry for you —2) To feel embarrassed

dar(le) pendiente a (alguien) (v.) —To make (someone) nervous ▪ *Me da mucho pendiente que mi nieto viaje solo.* I'm very worried about my grandchild traveling alone.

dar (algo) por hecho (v.) —To take (something) for granted ▪ *Yo sé que Ruperto prometió darte un aumento. Pero no lo des por hecho.* I know Ruperto promised to give you a raise. Just don't take it for granted.

dar(se) por ofendido (v.) —To take offense ▪ *Tu hermano se da por ofendido fácilmente.* Your brother takes offense very easily.

dar (algo) por sentado (v.) —To take (something) for granted

dar(le) por su lado a (alguien) (v.) —To humor (someone); to go along with (someone) ▪ *Yo sé que mi tía es muy rara. Dale por su lado y todo saldrá mejor.* I know my aunt is kind of weird. Just humor her a little and everything will be fine.

dar(se) por vencido (v.) —To give up ▪ *No puedo encontrar el error. Me doy por vencido.* I can't find the mistake. I give up.

dar(le) puerta a (alguien) (v.) —(slang) To flirt; to invite advances; also used when a girl allows her panties to show, whether intentionally or not ▪ *Esa chava me está dando puerta. That girl is giving me the come-on.*

dar(le) sabor al caldo (v.) —To make things interesting (*lit.* to give the broth some taste)

dar(le) sonaja a (alguien) (v.) —*(Mex)* (slang) To kill; to finish off; to bump off (someone)

dar(se) sus vueltas (v.) —To drop in every now and then to check on (something) ▪ *Vete tranquilo. Yo me voy a estar dando mis vueltas. You go ahead and leave without worrying. I'll be coming around to check up on the place.*

dar(se) taco (v.) —To be conceited or snotty

dar(le) trabajo a (alguien) (v.) —To be difficult ▪ *Le da mucho trabajo leer de corrido. It's not easy for him to read without stumbling over the words.*

dar(se) un agarrón con (alguien) (v.) —To have an intense but brief confrontation or fight with (someone) ▪ *Rodrigo se dio un agarrón con el gerente. Rodrigo and the manager had an ugly argument.*

dar(le) un aventón a (alguien) (v.) —To give (someone) a ride (*lit.* to push someone)

dar(le) un guamazo a (alguien) (v.) —*(Mex)* (slang) To give (someone) a terrific blow (purely physical)

dar(le) un jaloncito a (alguien) (v.) —*(Gua)* (slang) To give (someone) a ride

dar un mal paso (v.) —To get pregnant as a result of an affair; to get knocked up

dar(le) un norte a (alguien) (v.) —To give (someone) directions to get somewhere or to explain how to do something

dar(se) un pasón (v.) —(slang) To smoke a joint

dar(se) un pegue (v.) —(slang) To smoke a joint

dar(le) un plantón a (alguien) (v.) —To stand (someone) up; to keep (someone) waiting (*lit.* to plant someone)

dar(le) un sablazo a (alguien) (v.) —To hit up (someone) for a loan ▪ *Necesito dinero para el fin de semana. Voy a tener que darle un sablazo a mi papá. I need some money for the weekend. I think I'll hit up my dad for a loan.*

dar(se) un toque (v.) —(slang) To smoke a joint

dar(le) una coima a (alguien) (v.) —*(Arg, Bol)* (slang) To bribe

dar(le) una sopa de su propio chocolate a (alguien) (v.) —To give (someone) a taste of his own medicine (*lit.* to give someone a soup of his own chocolate)

dar(se) una vuelta (v.) —To visit; to drop in; to drop by (*lit.* to give yourself a turn) ▪ *Date una vuelta cuando salgas del trabajo, ¿sí? Drop in when you get off work, OK?*

dar(le) vuelo a la hilacha (v.) —(slang) To really let go and do (something) uninhibitedly

dar(le) vuelta a la tortilla (v.) —*(Mex)* (slang) To give (something) a rest; to forget it (*lit.* to turn the tortilla over) ▪ *Tengo años oyendo la misma queja. ¡Ya dale vuelta a la tortilla! I've been hearing the same complaint for years. Give it a rest!!*

dar(le) vueltas (a una idea) (v.) —To think (something) over carefully; to have irons in the fire; to consider a project (*lit.* to turn an idea over and over)

de ahí que ... —Therefore; so that is why ...

de aquí pa'l real (adv.) —*(Mex)* (slang) The rest is duck soup (easy); the rest is a breeze

de buena gana (adv.) —Willingly; gladly ▪ *Mi mamá siempre me ayuda de buena gana. No me hace un tango como tú. My mother always helps me quite willingly. She doesn't make a to-do about it, like you do.*

de buenas a primeras (adv.) —Without warning; suddenly; out of the blue ▪ *De buenas a primeras agarró sus chivas y se fue. Out of the clear blue sky he packed up and left.*

de (pura) casualidad (adv.) —By chance ▪ *¿De pura casualidad tienes un diskette? Do you by any chance have a diskette?*

de cualquier forma (manera; modo) (adv.) —Anyway

de chiripa (adv.) —By chance or coincidence ▪ *No se jugar dominó. Gané el juego de chiripa. I don't know how to play dominoes. I won by chance.*

de día y de noche (adv.) —Day in and day out

de (X momento) en adelante (adv.) —From (X moment) on; in the future ...

de entrada por salida (adv.) —1) In a rush ▪ *Pasé a su casa de entrada por salida. I dropped in, but didn't stay.* —2) Coming in every day but not spending the night (said of domestic help)

de golpe (y porrazo) (adv.) —*(Mex)* Suddenly

de gorra (adv.) —(slang) Free; without paying ▪ *A ver si podemos entrar al juego de gorra. Let's see if we can get into the game without buying a ticket.*

---

de hoquis (adv.) —(slang) Free

de igual a igual (adv.) —On the same footing ▪ *Yo quisiera poder hablar con mi hermano mayor de igual a igual.* I would like to speak to my elder brother on the same footing (as equals).

de la nada (adv.) —Out of thin air

de la patada (adv.) (adj.) —(slang) Very bad; very badly ▪ *Desde que me salí de esa empresa me está yendo de la patada.* Since I left that company I've been having a terrible time of it. *No me digas que invitaste a Gerardo a jugar golf. Juega de la patada.* Don't tell me you invited Gerardo to play golf. He plays a lousy game.

De la vista nace el amor —To see it is to love it

de lo lindo (adv.) —Very pleasantly or pleasurably ▪ *Fue una fiesta maravillosa. ¡Cantamos y bailamos de lo lindo!* It was a great party. We had a lot of fun singing and dancing!

de mala gana (adv.) —Reluctantly; grudgingly ▪ *El nuevo mozo hace todo de mala gana.* The new houseboy does everything very grudgingly.

de manera que … (adv.) —So; therefore

de maravilla (adv.) —Wonderfully well

de mi cuenta corre que … —I'll see to it that … ▪ *De mi cuenta corre que antes de una semana tienes trabajo.* I'll see to it that you have work before the week is out.

¡De ninguna manera!; ¡Ni pensarlo! (adv.) —No way!; It's unthinkable!; It's out of the question!

de perdida (de perdis) (adv.) —(slang) If nothing better can be arranged ▪ *De perdida devuélvame lo que pagué.* At least give me back what I paid.

de plano (adv.) —Simply; absolutely; no two ways about it ▪ *No insistas. De plano no voy.* Don't insist. I won't go, and that's that.

de por sí (adv.) —As it is; as things are; anyway; already; without any further aggravation ▪ *¿Cómo se te ocurre traer otro perro a la casa? De por sí no podemos alimentar a los que tenemos.* Are you crazy bringing home another dog? As it is, we can't feed the ones we have.

de puro churro (adv.) —(Mex) (slang) By chance or coincidence ▪ *Dio en el blanco de puro churro.* He hit the target by sheer chance.

de repente (adv.) —Suddenly

de su (mi, tu) cosecha (adv.) —(Mex) (something) of (someone's) invention (creation, making) ▪ *Este platillo no lo vas a encontrar en* *ningún recetario. Es de mi cosecha. You won't find this dish in any cook-book. It's my own invention.*

de su (mi, tu) puño y letra (adv.) —In (someone's) own handwriting

de un hilo (adv.) —Nonstop ▪ *Ha estado lloviendo de un hilo toda la semana. It has been raining nonstop for a week.*

de una vez por todas (adv.) —Once and for all

decir(le) (una; sus) fresca(s) a (alguien) (v.) —To give (someone) a piece of your mind; to tell (someone) off; to cuss each other out ▪ *Pedro y su cuñado se dijeron sus frescas. Pedro and his brother-in-law cussed each other out.*

decir(le) hasta la despedida a (alguien) (v.) —To tell (someone) off in no uncertain terms; to let (someone) have it ▪ *El jefe está colgado de la lámpara. Me dijo hasta la despedida. The boss is having kittens. He bawled the hell out of me.*

decir macanas (v.) —*(Arg)* (slang) To lie; to tell lies

decir pura cabeza de pescado (v.) —*(Chi)* (slang) To talk nonsense; to talk a lot of hot air ▪ *El orador se la pasó diciendo pura cabeza de pescado. The speaker talked a lot of nonsense.*

decir tallas (v.) —*(Chi)* (slang) To tell jokes

dejar a (alguien o algo) a la buena de Dios (v.) —To leave (someone or something) to chance; to neglect (someone or something)

dejar con la boca abierta (boquiabierto(a)) a (alguien) (v.) —To take (someone's) breath away

dejar con un palmo de narices a (alguien) (v.) —To thumb your nose at (someone); to give (someone) the brush off

dejar chiflando en la loma a (alguien) (v.) —1) To pay no attention to (someone) —2) To abandon (someone)

dejar dicho (v.) —1) *(Mex)* (slang) To leave word —2) *(Mex)* To leave money (an expression designed to avoid the word "money") ▪ *Si quieres que compre cervezas, "deja dicho." If you want me to buy some beer for you, leave money!*

dejar plantado(a) a (alguien) (v.) —To stand (someone) up

dejar que se (le) suban los humos a la cabeza a (alguien) (v.) —To be (to get) too big for your britches

dejar vestida(o) y alborotada(o) a (alguien) (v.) —To leave (someone) all dressed up with nowhere to go; to be stood up by some man (*lit.* to leave a woman all dressed up and excited)

---

desconchinflar(se) (v.) —(slang) To break down; to go on the blink
■ *La cafetera se desconchinfló. Nada más hay café soluble.* The coffeemaker is on the blink. There's only instant coffee.

descubrir el hilo negro (v.) —To feel that you have made an important discovery, when it's actually nothing new (*lit.* to discover black thread)

deschongar a (alguien) (v.) —To rough (someone) up in a brawl (*lit.* to mess up (someone's) hair bun by grabbing and twisting it in a fight)

¡Desde luego! —Of course!

desgarriate (n.) —*(Mex)* (slang) A mess ■ *Tu escritorio es un desgarriate.* Your desk is a mess.

deshacer(se) de (alguien o algo) (v.) —To get rid of (someone or something) ■ *Deberíamos deshacernos de ese sofá tan feo.* We should get rid of that ugly old sofa.

desliz (n.) —A torrid and short-lived affair, such as a one-night stand (said of a woman only) ■ *El bebé de Carmen es producto de un desliz.* Carmen's baby is the result of an affair.

despelote (n.) —*(Arg)* (slang) A mess; a situation that is out of control

despepitar (v.) —(slang) To talk; to sing (provide information)

despiporre (n.) —*(Mex)* (slang) A very noisy party; a mess

después de todo ... (adv.) —After all ...

destape (n.) —*(Mex)* Announcement of a party's candidate for president (or state governor)

destartalado(a) (adj.) —Old and the worse for wear; dilapidated

detallar(se) (v.) —*(Gua)* To kiss; to smooch

dilatar(se) (mucho) (v.) —*(Ven, Mex)* To be delayed or take a long time to get back or to do (something) ■ *Se dilataron en volver.* They took a long time to get back.

discutir pequeñeces (v.) —To split hairs

disparar(le) (algo) a (alguien) (v.) —*(Mex)* To be magnanimous about treating people to drink, meals, etc. ■ *¡Dispárame una cerveza!* Treat me to a beer!

doblar(se) de risa (v.) —To die laughing (*lit.* to double up in laughter)

doblar las manos (v.) —To give in (*lit.* to fold your hands)

dominar(se) (v.) —To control yourself; to get hold of yourself

dominguero(a) (adj.) —1) Sunday best —2) Used to describe a highfalutin word not always understood by ordinary people ▪ *El orador empleó palabras domingueras.* *The speaker used very highfalutin words.*

donde el aire da vuelta (adv.) —In the back of beyond; at the ends of the earth (*lit.* where the wind turns)

donde San Pedro perdió el guarache (adv.) —*(Mex)* (slang) In the back of beyond; at the ends of the earth (*lit.* where St. Peter lost his sandal)

dormir a pierna suelta (v.) —To sleep like a log (*lit.* to sleep with your legs all spread out)

dormir la mona (v.) —To sleep it off (when drunk)

echador (n.) (adj.) —*(Mex)* A boastful loudmouth

echar(se) a perder (v.) —1) To spoil ▪ *Si llevas a tu mamá, va a echar a perder la fiesta. If you take your mother, she's going to spoil the party.* —2) To spoil (to go bad) (intransitive) ▪ *La papaya se echó a perder. The papaya has spoiled (gone bad).* —3) To screw something up ▪ *Ya casi la había convencido cuando te metiste. ¡Echaste todo a perder! I had almost persuaded her when you barged in. You really screwed it up!*

echar(le) aguas a (alguien) (v.) —*(Mex)* (slang) To warn; to tell (someone) when it's OK to move or do (something) ▪ *Yo te echo aguas por si alguien viene. I'll stand lookout in case someone comes along.*

echar ajos y cebollas (v.) —To curse

echar de cabeza a (alguien) (v.) —To make (someone) look bad by revealing a secret about him or her ▪ *¿Por qué le dijiste a Flora lo que pienso de ella? ¡Me echaste de cabeza! Why did you tell Flora how I think about her? You made me look awful!*

echar de menos a (alguien) (v.) —To miss (someone) ▪ *Voy a echarte de menos. I'm gonna miss you.*

echar en cara (v.) —To remind (someone) of (something) very unpleasant he/she is or has done ▪ *Le echó en cara su cobardía. She taunted him with his cowardice.*

echar (algo) en saco roto (v.) —To ignore advice; to let (something) go in one ear and out the other (*lit.* to put (something) into a sack with a hole in it) ▪ *Acuérdate de lo que te dije. No lo eches en saco roto. Remember what I said. Don't just dismiss it.*

echar flores a (alguien) (v.) —To flatter or compliment (someone) (*lit.* to throw flowers at someone) ▪ *Pancho siempre me echa muchas flores. Pancho always flatters me a lot.*

echar la casa por la ventana (v.) —To go the whole hog; to go all out (*lit.* to throw the house out the window) ▪ *Se casa su única hija. Va a echar la casa por la ventana. His only daughter is getting married. He's going to go all out.*

echar(le) la viga a (alguien) (v.) —*(Mex)* (slang) To bawl the hell out of (someone) (*lit.* to throw the beam at someone) ▪ *Me echó la viga. Estaba enojadísimo. He was really mad. He bawled the hell out of me.*

echar(le) leña al fuego (v.) —To add fuel to the fire; to pour oil on the flames ▪ *No vayas a preguntarle al Sr. Roberts por su esposa. Sería como echarle leña al fuego. Don't ask Mr. Roberts about his wife. You'll just* *add fuel to the fire.*

echar(le) los kilos (v.) —To do (something) with the utmost of enthusiasm ▪ **Debemos tener listos los informes para las 12:00. ¡Échale los kilos!** *The reports have to be ready by twelve. Put all you've got into it.*

echar(le) los perros a (alguien) (v.) —*(Mex)* (slang) To flirt with (someone); to make a pass at (someone) *(lit.* to set the dogs on someone) ▪ **Ese tipo le está echando los perros a mi hermana.** *That guy is coming on to my sister.*

echar(le) montón a (algo) (v.) —*(Mex)* To pitch in together to get (something) done ▪ **Terminamos rápido, porque le echamos montón al trabajo.** *We finished quickly, because we pitched in together to get it over with.*

echar(le) montón a (alguien) (v.) —*(Mex)* To gang up on (someone) ▪ **Esos cobardes me echaron montón.** *Those cowards ganged up on me.*

echar paja (v.) —*(Col)* (slang) To lie; to tell a lie

echar pestes de (alguien) (v.) —To badmouth (someone) ▪ **¿Qué le hiciste a tu suegra? Está echando pestes de ti.** *What did you do to your mother-in-law? She's saying the most awful things about you.*

echar por tierra (algo) (v.) —To throw cold water on (something)

echar relajo (v.) —*(Mex)* (slang) To fool around noisily; to joke around; to have a lot of noisy fun ▪ **El equipo de basket venía echando mucho relajo en el avión.** *The basketball team was very rowdy on the plane.*

echar (un) rollo (v.) —(slang) To go into a great deal of confusing and roundabout detail about something, intentionally or not ▪ **Tengo prisa. ¿No puedes explicarlo sin echar tanto rollo?** *I'm in a hurry. Can't you explain it in a less roundabout way?*

echar taco de ojo (v.) —*(Mex)* (slang) To get an eyeful of a good-looking babe or guy ▪ **Cada vez que pasa la nueva secre, Mauricio se echa su taco de ojo.** *Every time the new secretary goes by, Mauricio ogles her.*

echar(le) tierra a (alguien) (v.) —To badmouth (someone) ▪ **Este gobernador le echó tierra al anterior.** *The present governor said all kinds of awful things about the previous governor.*

echar(le) tierra a (algo) (v.) —To hush something up ▪ **Hay que echarle tierra al incidente antes de que regrese el jefe.** *We have to hush up the incident before the boss comes back.*

echar(se) un farolazo (v.) —*(Mex)* (slang) To have a shot (a drink); to knock one back

echar(le) un fon a (alguien) (v.) —(slang) To give (someone) a ring

(telephone call)

echar(se) un mechazo (v.) —*(Gua)* (slang) To have a shot (a drink); to knock one back

echar(le) un ojo al gato y otro al garabato (v.) —To be alert to two things at the same time; to be on your toes

echar(se) un palo (v.) —1) *(Ven)* (slang) To have a shot (a drink) ▪ *No bebo mucho, pero de vez en cuando me echo mis palitos. I don't drink much, but I'll have a little something every now and then.* —2) *(Mex)* (very vulgar) To have sex (from **echar(se)** (slang): to have and **palo**: stick)

echar(se) un pencazo (v.) —*(Chi)* (slang) To have a shot (a drink); to knock one back

echar(se) un taco (v.) —*(Mex)* (slang) To have (something) to eat on the go

echar(le) un torito a (alguien) (v.) —(slang) To throw out a hard question (*lit.* to throw a little bull)

echar(le) una mano a (alguien) (v.) —To lend (someone) a hand ▪ *Échame una mano con mi tarea. Give me a hand with my homework.*

embejucar(se) (v.) —*(Col)* (slang) To get all mixed up

embolar(se) (v.) —*(Gua)* (slang) To get drunk

embullar (v.) —*(CA, Ant)* (slang) To get all excited about (something) ▪ *Estoy embullado con el proyecto. I'm all excited about the project.*

empachecar(se) (v.) —*(Ven)* (slang) To feel that you're freezing

emperifollado(a) (adj.) —Dressed to kill, particularly when it involves a complicated hairdo

empinar el codo (v.) —(slang) To drink (*lit.* to bend your elbow)

en casa del diablo (adv.) —In the back of beyond; at the ends of the earth (*lit.* at the Devil's house) ▪ *Le dije a Alberto que le daba un aventón, pero no sabía que vive en casa del diablo. I told Alberto I'd give him a ride, but I didn't know he lives in the back of beyond.*

en cuanto (adv.) —As soon as ▪ *Avísame en cuanto llegues. Let me know as soon as you get there.*

en el fin del mundo (adv.) —At the ends of the earth

en el quinto infierno (adv.) —In the back of beyond; at the ends of the earth (*lit.* in the fifth hell)

¡En la torre! —*(Mex)* Gosh!; Hell!; How awful!

en limpio (adv.) —Said of the final, corrected, clean version of something written ▪ *Ya revisé la carta. Ahora pásala en limpio. I read the let-*

ter. Now you have to type it up.

en línea recta (adv.) —As the crow flies (*lit.* in a straight line)

en pocas palabras (adv.) —In a nutshell

en un dos por tres (adv.) —In two shakes of a lamb's tail; in a flash; in no time at all

en una de ésas (adv.) —One of these days; on one of those attempts; by sheer chance ■ *En una de ésas le atinas. Eventually (on one of your tries), you'll get it right (by sheer chance).*

en virtud de (adv.) —Due to; because of

encajar(se) (v.) —(slang) To take unfair advantage of (someone) ■ *Se encajaron con el precio. They went overboard with the price.*

encamotar(se) (v.) —*(Mex)* (slang) To be all mixed up ■ *Estoy encamotado con las cuentas. I got all mixed up with the accounts.*

encargar (v.) —*(Mex)* To get pregnant ■ *Luisa encargó al año de casada. Luisa got pregnant one year after her wedding.*

encargar(le) (algo) a (alguien) (v.) —To ask (someone) to do something ■ *Vine porque tu jefe me encargó que pasara a recogerlo. I came because your boss asked me to come pick him up.*

encargar(se) del changarro (v.) —*(Mex)* To mind the store (*lit.* to look after the store) ■ *Tengo que ir al banco. Encárgate del changarro, por favor. I have to go to the bank. Mind the store, will you?*

encontrar(le) el modo a (algo o alguien) (v.) —To get the hang of (someone or something) ■ *Leobardo es un gruñón contigo, pero yo ya le encontré el modo. Leobardo is a grump with you, but I've figured out how to treat him. Ayúdame a encontrarle el modo a esta copiadora. Yo sé que funciona. Help me figure out how to get this copier going. I know it works.*

encontrar la horma de su zapato (v.) —To meet your match

encuetar(se) (v.) —*(Mex)* (slang) To get drunk

enchinar(sele) el cuero (v.) —(slang) To get goose bumps from cold or fear ■ *Salí del agua y se me enchinó el cuero. I got out of the water and got goose bumps.*

enchinchar a (alguien) (v.) —1) (slang) To bother (someone) ■ *No me estés enchinchando ahorita. Tengo que terminar este informe. Don't bother me now. I have to finish this report.* —2) To waste (someone's) time

engavetado(a) (adj.) —*(ES)* (slang) (something) that has been hushed up ■ *Ahora nadie sabe que estuvo en la cárcel. Ese asunto ha sido engavetado. The matter of his time in jail has been hushed up. Nobody knows* *about it now.*

enseñar el cobre (v.) —To show your true colors (*lit.* to show the copper; from silver or gold-plated copper, when the plating wears thin, the copper shows through) ▪ **El novio de mi hermana enseñó el cobre cuando supo que estaba embarazada.** *My sister's boyfriend showed his true colors when he found out that she was pregnant.*

¡Entrale! —*(Mex)* Dig in!

entre pitos y flautas (adv.) —What with one thing and another (*lit.* with whistles and flutes) ▪ **Entre pitos y flautas, el viaje costó cerca de 5,000 dólares.** *What with one thing and another, the trip cost close to 5,000 dollars.*

entre que son peras o son manzanas (adv.) —Until this can be cleared up or figured out ▪ **No nos mandaron el desglose de la factura, pero entre que son peras o son manzanas, hay que pagarla.** *They didn't provide a breakdown of the invoice, but in the meantime, it has to be paid.*

envainar(se) (v.) —*(Col)* (slang) To get into hot water

enverracar(se) (v.) —*(Col)* (slang) To get very mad at (someone) ▪ **Juan se enverracó con su hermana.** *Juan is very mad at his sister.*

¡Es de ley! (adv.) —*(Ecu)* It's a must!

¡Es un quilombo! —*(Arg)* (slang) It's a mess!

escabechar(se) a (alguien) (v.) —*(Mex)* (slang) To kill (someone) ▪ **Por fin se escabecharon al bravucón ése.** *They finally bumped off that thug.*

escuincle(a) (escuintle(a)) (n.) (adj.) —*(Mex)* Youngster (from the **Nahuatl Itzcuintle**, small dog of pre-Columbian times)

escupir los hígados (v.) —(slang) To be worn to a frazzle (*lit.* to spit out your livers) ▪ **Juan subió las cajas solo. Está escupiendo los hígados.** *Juan carried up the boxes all by himself. He's worn to a frazzle.*

escurrir el bulto (v.) —Not to face something; to wriggle out from under (something) ▪ **El responsable del fracaso está escurriendo el bulto.** *The person responsible for the failure of the venture is trying to slither out from under it (pretend he has nothing to do with it).*

eso es coche de otro chiquero (v.) —*(Gua)* That's another kettle of fish; that's a horse of a different color

eso es gallo de otro gallinero (v.) —*(Cuba)* That's another kettle of fish; that's a horse of a different color

eso es harina de otro costal (v.) —That's another kettle of fish; that's a horse of a different color

eso es sapo de otro pozo (v.) —*(Arg)* That's another kettle of fish;

that's a horse of a different color

¡Está de morirse! —*(CR)* This (it, that) is to die for!

estar a la cuarta pregunta (v.) —To be broke

estar a la disposición de (alguien) (v.) —To be at (someone's) beck and call

estar a medio palo (v.) —*(Ven)* To be a bit drunk

estar a medios chiles (v.) —*(Mex)* (slang) To be a bit drunk

estar a punto de ... (v.) —To be about to (do something) ▪ *El pobre de mi hermano está a punto de volverse loco con tanto trabajo.* My poor brother is about to go crazy with so much work.

estar abusado(a) (v.) —*(Mex)* (slang) To get or to be on the alert for an opportunity or eventuality ▪ *Si quieres la beca, tienes que estar muy abusado en el examen.* If you want this scholarship, you really have to be on the ball during the test.

estar adelantado (el reloj) (v.) —Said when a watch or clock is fast ▪ *Tu reloj está adelantado.* Your watch is fast.

estar agotado(a) (v.) —1) To be worn out; to be exhausted ▪ *Caminé un par de horas. Estoy agotado.* I walked for a couple of hours. I'm exhausted. —2) To be out of stock ▪ *Lo siento señor. Este libro está agotado.* I'm sorry sir. We're out of this book.

estar al corriente de (algo) (v.) —To be up-to-date with (something) ▪ *No estoy al corriente del pago de impuestos.* I'm not up-to-date with my taxes.

estar al tanto (v.) —To be up on something; to be informed about (something) ▪ *¿Estás al tanto de lo que está pasando en la Bolsa?* Are you up-to-date on what's happening at the stock exchange?

estar amasijado(a) (v.) —*(Arg)* (slang) To be worn out; to be exhausted

estar apachurrado(a) (v.) —To be down in the dumps

estar batallando (v.) —To struggle with something ▪ *Juan está batallando para poder pagar el coche.* Juan is having trouble paying for the car.

estar bueno(a) (v.) —(slang, vulgar) To be really very physically attractive ▪ *¡Esa vieja está muy buena!* That broad is hot.

estar caliente (v.) —(quite vulgar) To be horny

estar canijo (v.) —*(Mex)* (slang) To be tough, difficult to deal with ▪ *Va a estar canijo hacerlo en tan poco tiempo.* It's going to be practically impossible to do it in such a short time.

estar color de hormiga (v.) —*(ES, Mex)* To be very difficult (situations) ■ *Por tu culpa, la cosa está color de hormiga. The situation got very difficult, thanks to you.*

estar como agua para (pa') chocolate (v.) —*(Mex)* To be absolutely furious (*lit.* to be as hot as the water needed to melt chocolate)

estar como boca de lobo (v.) —To be as black as night (for places, not things or people)

estar con el agua hasta el cuello (v.) —To be in hot water; to be up to here; to be at the breaking point (*lit.* to have the water level up to your neck)

estar con el pendiente (v.) —To worry; to be concerned ■ *Elisa está con el pendiente porque Jorge dijo que llegaba a las seis, pero no aparece. Elisa is worried because Jorge said he'd be here at six, but he hasn't showed up.*

estar crudo(a) (v.) —*(Mex)* (slang) To have a hangover (*lit.* to be raw)

estar cursiento(a) (v.) —*(Mex)* To have the runs (diarrhea)

estar de adorno (v.) —To be useless for a specific purpose; to serve only as a decoration ■ *El gerente no sirve, nomás está de adorno. The manager is a dolt. He's just there as a decoration.*

estar de capa caída (v.) —To be somewhat depressed, downhearted (*lit.* to go around with your cape drooping)

estar (ser) de fábula (v.) —To be fabulous (fantastic, terrific)

estar de miedo (v.) —*(Chi)* To be super ■ *¿Ya viste el nuevo Golf? ¡Está de miedo! Have you seen the new Golf? It's terrific!*

estar empapado(a) en (X) (v.) —To be very knowledgeable or have a lot of information about (something) ■ *Pregúntale a Mario, él está empapado en el asunto. Ask Mario. He has all the dope on this matter.*

estar en cueros (v.) —To be (or run around) naked ■ *Ahorita no te puedo abrir. Estoy en cueros. I can't open for you right now. I'm not dressed.*

estar en chino (v.) —*(Mex)* To be very difficult ■ *¿Quieres que venda todas las llantas hoy mismo? ¡Está en chino! You want me to sell all the tires today? Get real!*

estar en estado (v.) —(slang) To be pregnant ■ *Cuando está en estado tiene náuseas. She feels nauseated when she's pregnant.*

estar en la baba (v.) —*(Mex)* (slang) To be off in a cloud; to be daydreaming (*lit.* to be drooling)

estar en la olla (v.) —*(Col, Mex)* To be broke

estar en las nubes (v.) —To be off on a cloud (*lit.* to be in the clouds)

estar encariñado(a) con (alguien o algo) (v.) —To have a soft spot for (someone or something) ▪ *Mi esposa está muy encariñada con ese perrito callejero.* My wife really has a soft spot for that little street dog.

estar entrado(a) con (algo) (v.) —To be really hooked on something ▪ *Alicia está muy entrada con la telenovela.* Alicia is really hooked on the soap opera.

estar entre (algo) (v.) —*(Gua)* To be inside something ▪ *¡Búscalo! Está entre mi bolsa.* Look for it! It's in my purse.

estar forrado(a) de billetes (v.) —To be filthy rich; to have money coming out your ears (*lit.* to be lined with bills)

estar frío(a) (v.) —*(Mex)* To be broke ▪ *Pagué la comida y me quedé frío.* I was broke after I paid for the lunch.

estar frito(a) (v.) —*(Mex)* To be up a creek without a paddle ▪ *La llave se quedó encerrada en el coche. ¡Ahora sí que estamos fritos!* The keys are locked in the car. Now we're really in trouble!

estar grueso(a) (v.) —1) *(Mex)* To be difficult (situation) ▪ *¿Quieres que pague seis mensualidades por adelantado? ¡Está grueso!* You want me to pay six installments in advance? Practically impossible! —2) To be so good or so bad that it's hard to equal (people) ▪ *Lalo tiene a tres chavas embarazadas. ¡Está grueso!* Lalo has got three girls pregnant. Incredible! *Ana se ganó cuatro medallas en los juegos olímpicos. ¡Está gruesa!* Ana won four Olympic medals. Fantastic!

estar hecho(a) bolas (v.) —To be confused

estar hecho(a) (un) camote (v.) —*(Mex)* (slang) To be all mixed up ▪ *Estoy hecho un camote con las cuentas.* I'm confused about the accounts.

estar hecho(a) un brazo de mar (v.) —To be enraged; in a state; fit to be tied

estar hecho(a) un reo (v.) —*(Arg)* (slang) To be poorly dressed ▪ *No le perdono que haya llegado a mi fiesta hecho un reo.* I will never forgive him for turning up at my party so badly dressed.

estar hinchado(a) de dinero (v.) —To be filthy rich; to have money coming out your ears (*lit.* to be swollen with money)

estar ladrando (v.) —*(Ven)* To be broke

estar lejos de (v.) —To be a far cry from ▪ *La comida de este restaurante está lejos de ser lo que era cuando venía con mi papá.* The food at this restaurant is a far cry from what it was when I used to come with my father.

estar limpio(a) (v.) —*(Ven)* To be broke

---

estar malogrado(a) (v.) —*(Peru)* To be out of order

estar mortal (v.) —*(CR)* To be very good (things only) ▪ *¡Este tamal está mortal! This tamale is marvelous!*

estar muerto(a) (v.) —To be worn out; to be exhausted ▪ *Estoy muerto de cansancio. I'm dead tired.*

estar padre (adv.) —*(Mex)* To be great (wonderful, marvelous, terrific) ▪ *¡Esta oficina está muy padre! This office is just great!*

estar para el arrastre (v.) —To be in a terrible state; to be completely worn out and beat up (from bullfighting; the dead bull is dragged out of the ring) ▪ *Ese cuate está para el arrastre. That guy has had it!*

estar para llorar (v.) —*(Mex)* To be pathetically awful (*lit.* to make you break down and cry) ▪ *Ese cuadro está para llorar. That painting is simply dreadful!*

estar pasado(a) (v.) —1) To be spoiled or too ripe (food) —2) To be high on drugs

estar pelado(a) (v.) —*(Chi)* (slang) To be broke

estar pelón (pelona) (v.) —1) To be hairless ▪ *La quimo lo dejó pelón. The chemotherapy left him bald.* —2) (slang) To be difficult ▪ *Está pelón ganarte al póker. It's practically impossible to beat you at poker.*

estar plagado(a) de (algo) (v.) —(slang) To have too many or too much of (something) or to be overrun by (something) ▪ *El texto está plagado de errores. The text is full of mistakes. Acapulco está plagado de turistas. Acapulco is crawling with tourists.*

estar podrido(a) (v.) —*(Arg)* (slang) To be fed up (*lit.* to be rotten) ▪ *¡Gracias a Dios que llegaste! Estoy podrido de esperarte. Thank God you're here at last! I'm sick to death of waiting for you.*

estar por (+ verb) (v.) —To be about to do (something) ▪ *Estamos por empezar la junta. We're about to start the meeting.*

estar por los suelos (adv.) —1) To be down in the dumps; to be completely depressed —2) To be at rock bottom (*lit.* to be on the floor)

estar (muy) puesto(a) (v.) —*(Mex)* To be very keen or gung ho about something ▪ *La fiesta es el jueves. Mauricio está muy puesto. The party is on Thursday. Mauricio is really looking forward to it.*

estar que arde (v.) —To be hot; to sizzle (*lit.* to be burning) ▪ *Acusaron al gerente de fraude. ¡La cosa está que arde! The manager has been accused of fraud. The situation is sizzling!*

estar rendido(a) (v.) —To be worn out; to be exhausted

estar seco(a) (v.) —*(Arg)* (slang) To be broke

estar vivito(a) y coleando (v.) —To be alive and kicking (*lit.* to be alive and wagging your tail)

estirar la pata (v.) —To kick the bucket (*lit.* to stretch out your leg)

F

fajar(se) (v.) —To work really hard; to fight really hard ▪ *Tuvimos que fajarnos toda la noche, pero sacamos el trabajo.* *We had to work like crazy all night long, but we got all the work done.*

fajar(se) a (alguien) (v.) —(slang) To neck; to indulge in heavy petting

fajar(se) los pantalones (v.) —To get strict; to put your foot down; to get tough ▪ *Mi hijo va de mal en peor. Voy a tener que fajarme los pantalones con él.* *My son is going from bad to worse. I'm going to have to get tough with him.*

falso cumplido (n.) —A left-handed compliment

fanfarrón (fanfarrona) (n.) —*(Ven, Mex, Arg)* A loudmouth show-off

faramalla (n.) —1) *(Mex)* (slang) A big to-do; a lot of noise —2) *(Ven)* A boastful loudmouth

fayuca (n.) —(slang) Contraband; goods smuggled into the country without paying duties

feria (n.) —*(CR)* Lagniappe; bonus; gratuity; baker's dozen

ferrocarril (n.) —*(Uru)* A crib sheet; secret notes to copy from in a test (*lit.* railroad)

finado(a) (n.) (adj.) —*(Chi, Mex, Uru)* Deceased; dearly departed ▪ *Mi finado esposo.* *My late husband.*

fregar a (alguien) (v.) —*(ES, Mex)* (vulgar) To bother (someone)

fregón (fregona) (n.) (adj.) —1) (vulgar) A person who is the best at something or at everything ▪ *Sergio acaba de ganar dos mil pesos. Es un fregón en el póker.* *Sergio just won two thousand pesos at poker. He's the best!* —2) A person who is a pest

freguetas (n.) —A person who is a pest

fundillo (n.) —The human backside; the derrière (vulgar in Mexico)

G

gacho(a) (n.) (adj.) —*(Mex)* (slang) Not nice ▪ *Tu hermano es bien gacho. No me ayuda con mi tarea.* Your brother is really mean. He won't help me with my homework.

gago (n.) —*(Ven)* (slang) A person who stutters

galleta (n.) —*(Ven)* (slang) A mess; a messy situation

gandalla (n.) (adj.) —*(Mex)* (slang) Not a pal

gandul (n.) (adj.) —A lazy bum

gasfitero (n.) —*(Peru)* (slang) Man who installs and fixes gas heaters and stoves (from the British "gas fitter")

gil (n.) —*(Arg, Uru)* (slang) A dolt; a person who is not very bright

gila (n.) —*(Peru)* A girl in love

goma (n.) —*(Gua, CR)* (slang) Hangover

góndola (n.) —*(CR)* (slang) A bus

gorrear (gorronear) (v.) —(slang) To mooch off (someone)

gorrón (gorrona) (n.) (adj.) —A person who always mooches off others

(la) grilla (n.) —*(Mex)* (slang) Low, intriguing politics

gringo(a) (n.) (adj.) —(slang) A person or thing from the United States

gritos y sombrerazos —A big to-do; a ruckus; shouts and yells (of upset people); with a great hullabaloo; in an uproar (*lit.* shouting and hitting with the hat)

guacarear(se) (v.) —*(Mex)* (slang) To throw up

guacho (n.) —*(Arg)* (slang) Boy; orphan; young animal

guagua (n.) —*(Cuba)* (slang) Bus

guarandinga (n.) —*(Ven)* (slang) A thingamajig; a whatchamacallit

guarango (n.) (adj.) —*(Uru)* (slang) Rough; rude

guardar cama (v.) —To stay in bed ▪ *A causa de su embarazo tiene que guardar cama.* She has to stay in bed because of her pregnancy.

guardar las apariencias (v.) —To keep up appearances

guasabeo (n.) —*(Cuba)* (slang) The act of necking ▪ *Aquella pareja está en el guasabeo.* That couple is necking.

guayabo (n.) —1) A fruit tree —2) *(Col)* (slang) A hangover

guayoso(a) (n.) (adj.) —(slang) Complaining; said of a grouch or a person who crabs a lot

---

güero(a) (adj.) —*(Mex)* (slang) Blond; not dark-complexioned

guindar(se) (v.) —1) *(Cuba)* (slang) To kick the bucket —2) *(Ven)* To lie down; to go to bed; to hit the hay

güirigüiri (n.) —*(Mex)* (slang) Gossip and generally senseless talk; yack-ety-yak

¿Gusta? ¿Gustas? —Do you want some? Do you want to?

ha(n) de ser (X hora(s)) —Said when guessing what time it is ▪ *Han de ser como las siete. It must be around seven o'clock.*

haber mar de fondo (v.) —There's more to it than meets the eye ▪ *No se entienden las explicaciones que dieron. Aquí hay mar de fondo. Their explanations cannot be understood. There's more here than meets the eye.*

haber más capeadores que toros (v.) —*(CR)* There are too many cooks (*lit.* there are more bullfighters than bulls)

haber moros en la costa (v.) —The walls have ears (*lit.* there are Moors on the coast)

hablando del rey de Roma ... —Speaking of the devil ...

hablar de bulto (v.) —To gesticulate while talking

hablar hasta por los codos (v.) —To talk (someone's) ear off; to chatter; to talk too much (*lit.* to speak from all parts of your body, including your elbows)

hablar horrores de (alguien) (v.) —To badmouth (someone)

hablar paja (v.) —*(Ven)* (slang) To babble

hablar sin rodeos (v.) —To talk turkey

hacer(se) (v.) —(slang) To pee (more rarely: to poop); to wet your pants; to dirty your pants ▪ *Ya se hizo el niño. Hay que cambiarlo. The baby pooped. He has to be changed.*

hacer(se) ... (v.) —To play dumb ▪ *Tú lo tomaste. ¡No te hagas! You took it. Don't play dumb!*

hacer(se) a la idea (v.) —To get used to the idea ▪ *No me hago a la idea de que mi papá murió. I can't get used to the idea that my dad is dead.*

hacer(se) bolas (v.) —*(Mex)* To get all mixed up ▪ *No sólo no entendí, sino que con su explicación terminé hecho bolas. Not only did I not understand; his explanation mixed me up even worse.*

hacer(le) caso a (alguien o algo) (v.) —To heed or pay attention to (someone or something) ▪ *Hazle caso a tu padre. Pay attention to what your father says.*

hacer cola (v.) —To stand in line ▪ *Mireya y yo te esperamos allá. No todos tenemos que hacer cola. Mireya and I will wait for you over there. We don't all have to stand in line.*

hacer como que (+ verb) (v.) —To pretend that ... ▪ *Haz como que no lo ves. Pretend you don't see him.*

hacer corajes (v.) —To get really upset about (something) ▪ *Por favor, no discutas con Mamá. No debe hacer corajes. Please don't argue with Mother. She shouldn't get upset.*

hacer(se) cruces (v.) —To fail to understand something (*lit.* to cross yourself in the hope that God will help you to understand) ▪ *No entendió, se quedó haciéndose cruces. He didn't understand. He just sat there wondering what was going on.*

hacer de cuenta (v.) —To pretend; to imagine ▪ *Nunca has estado en la ciudad de Quebec, ¿verdad? Pues haz de cuenta una ciudad de Francia. You've never been to Quebec City, have you? Well, it's just like a city in France.*

hacer(la) de emoción (v.) —(*Mex*) To make a big deal out of something; to blow (something) out of proportion ▪ *¡No la hagas de emoción! Dime ya lo que pasó. Don't make such a big thing out of it! Just tell me what happened.*

hacer(se) de la vista gorda (v.) —To turn a blind eye ▪ *Mamá sabe que Julio fuma, pero se hace de la vista gorda. Mother knows Julio smokes but she just turns a blind eye.*

hacer(la) de tos (v.) —(*Mex*) (slang) To overdo or drag something out too long; to make a big thing of (something) ▪ *Llevas una hora sermoneando a la pobre de María. Ya no la hagas de tos. You've been preaching at poor Maria for one hour. Give it a rest. Nada más te dio un llegue con la defensa. No la hagas de tos. He just touched your car with his fender. Don't make a big thing out of it.*

hacer de tripas corazón (v.) —To get up the guts to do ▪ *Tuve que hacer de tripas corazón para entrar a pedir el aumento. I had to screw up my courage to go in and ask for a raise.*

hacer(le) el favor a (alguien) (v.) —1) To do a favor ▪ *Hágame (hazme) el favor de comprarme cigarros. Do me the favor of buying cigarettes for me.* —2) To take a girl to bed ▪ *Le hicieron el favor y está embarazada. Somebody took her to bed and now she's pregnant.*

hacer(le) el fuchi a (alguien o algo) (v.) —(*Mex*) To turn up your nose at (someone or something) ▪ *Carmen le hizo el fuchi a tu pastel. Carmen turned up her nose at your cake.*

hacer(se) el (la) interesante (v.) —To play hard to get

hacer(se) el (la) muerto(a) (v.) —(*Mex*) (slang) To play dumb, or to pretend you don't know or notice (something) because it would go against your interests to do so ▪ *Ponte con una lana para la colecta, Freddy. No te hagas el muerto. Pull out some money for the collection,*

Freddy. Don't play dead.

hacer(le) el vacío a (alguien) (v.) —To avoid (someone); to spurn (someone) ▪ *Jaime me hizo el vacío en la fiesta. ¿Sabes por qué? Jaime avoided me at the party. Any idea why?*

hacer falta (alguien o algo) (v.) —To lack; to have need of; to be missing ▪ *Todavía hace falta Berenice. Bernice is still missing. Aquí hacen falta más sillas. We need more chairs here.*

hacer(le) gracia a (alguien) (v.) —To be amusing ▪ *Este programa me hace mucha gracia. This TV show is very amusing.*

hacer juego con (algo) (v.) —To match ▪ *Tus zapatos no hacen juego con la bolsa. Your shoes don't match your handbag.*

hacer(le) la lucha a (algo) (v.) —To make a special effort ▪ *Yo sé que no es fácil llegar temprano, pero hazle la lucha, ¿no? I know it's not easy to get here early, but make an effort, will you?*

hacer las paces (v.) —To bury the hatchet ▪ *Ya estoy cansado de discutir contigo. Vamos a hacer las paces, ¿no? I'm tired of arguing with you. Let's bury the hatchet, OK?*

hacer(le) mala obra (v.) —To do (someone) a bad turn; to do a bad deed (to someone)

hacer(le) manita de puerco a (alguien) (v.) —*(Mex)* (slang) To twist (someone's) arm ▪ *Héctor no quería venir. Tuve que hacerle manita de puerco. Hector didn't want to come. I had to twist his arm.*

hacer (su) numerito (v.) —(slang) To do (something) ridiculous

hacer pantalla (pantallar) (v.) —*(Arg, Col, Cuba, Chi)* (slang) To impress ▪ *¡Me hizo pantalla con todos esos títulos! He impressed me with all those degrees!*

hacer (una) pataleta (v.) —To have a tantrum ▪ *La niña esta haciendo una pataleta porque le apagué la tele. The kid is having a tantrum because I turned off the TV.*

hacer(se) pelotas (v.) —(slang) To get all mixed up; to get confused

hacer pucheros (v.) —To screw up your mouth as if you're about to cry

hacer puente (v.) —*(Mex)* To take the day(s) off between a weekend and a holiday in order to make a long weekend of it ▪ *El día de la Independencia es el martes, y vamos a hacer puente desde el viernes hasta el siguiente miércoles. Independence day is on Tuesday, so we're going to take a long weekend from Friday to the following Wednesday.*

hacer(se) (del) rogar (v.) —To pretend to be reluctant, so that (some-

one) has to beg you to do (something) ■ *Celia dice que no quiere ir,*
pero sólo se está haciendo del rogar. *Celia says she doesn't want to go, but*
it's not true. She just wants us to beg her.

hacer San Lunes (v.) —*(Mex)* (slang) To take Monday off because the
weekend was too exhausting (*lit.* to celebrate St. Monday)

hacer talacha (v.) —*(Mex)* (slang) To change a tire; to do minor car
repairs or do minor handyman's jobs around the house

hacer(sele) un nudo en la garganta (v.) —To get a lump in your
throat ■ *Cuando me avisaron que había muerto, se me hizo un nudo en*
la garganta. *I got a lump in my throat when they told me she died.*

hacer una tempestad en un vaso de agua (v.) —To make a mountain out of a molehill (*lit.* to make a tempest in a glass of water)

hallar la horma de su zapato (v.) —To meet your match

hasta decir basta (adv.) —Used when people overdo (something) or
when (something) is in excess ■ *Cuando estuvimos en Veracruz, comi-*
mos mariscos hasta decir basta. *When we were in Veracruz, we ate seafood*
until it was coming out our ears.

hasta en la sopa (adv.) —Everywhere (*lit.* even in the soup) ■ *Veo a tu*
hermano hasta en la sopa. *I see your brother everywhere I turn.*

¡Hazme el favor! (¡Hágame el favor!) —What do you think of that?
(negative connotation) ■ *Le pegó sin motivo. ¡Hazme el favor!* *She*
whacked him for no reason. I ask you!!

hereje (adj.) —*(Ven)* (slang) Huge; enormous ■ *¡Tengo un sueño hereje!* *I*
am awfully sleepy.

¡Hijo! (¡Hijos!) (¡Híjole) —(slang) Gosh!; Golly!; Jeez!; Good God!;
Holy cow!

hocicón (hocicona) (n.) —1) (slang) A person who talks too much or
says too much —2) A liar (*lit.* having a snout)

¡Hombre! —1) Friend!; Buddy! —2) Certainly!

hoy por hoy (adv.) —Nowadays; at the present time

huacal (n.) —*(Mex)* A sort of crate made of thin peeled tree branches,
used since time immemorial in Mexico ■ *Trajo un huacal de tunas.* *He*
brought a crate of prickly pears.

huachafo (n.) —*(Peru)* (slang) A badly dressed person

huevón (huevona) (n.) (adj.) —1) *(CR)* (slang) A guy; buddy, chap
—2) *(Mex)* (very vulgar) Lazy bum

igualado(a) (adj.) —Not sufficiently respectful; too chummy

inflar (v.) —*(Mex)* (slang) To drink (*lit.* to inflate)

ingeniar(selas) para (algo) (v.) —To figure out how to ... ▪ *Se las ingenió para arreglar el coche él solo.* He figured out how to fix the car all by himself.

invento de hombre blanco (n.) —A new and unfamiliar machine or gadget that you're not sure how to use (*lit.* an invention of the white man)

ir(se) al diablo (demonio) (v.) —To go jump in the lake; to go to hell (*lit.* to go to the devil)

ir al tranco (v.) —*(Arg)* (slang) To go slowly (used mainly in reference to a horse)

ir(le) como en feria a (alguien) (v.) —*(Mex)* (slang) To have (something) very unpleasant happen to you ▪ *Por andar metiéndome con el grandulón ese, me fue como en feria.* I shouldn't have picked a fight with that big bruiser. He made me regret it.

ir(se) con la finta (v.) —To be taken in by (someone or something); to fall for (something) ▪ *Como traía muchas tarjetas de crédito y un coche bonito, me fui con la finta. Pensé que tenía dinero.* I saw he had a lot of credit cards and a nice car, and I was fooled. I thought he had money.

ir(se) con su música a otra parte (v.) —*(Mex)* To go bother (someone) elsewhere; to stop being a nuisance; to stop getting in the way (*lit.* to take your music somewhere else) ▪ *No tengo tiempo de oír tonterías. Vete con tu música a otra parte.* I don't have time to listen to nonsense. Go away and bother someone else.

ir de compras (v.) —To go shopping

ir(se) de espaldas (v.) —To fall over backwards in surprise or shock

ir de mal en peor (v.) —To go from bad to worse ▪ *No consigo trabajo y cada día me endeudo más. Las cosas van de mal en peor.* I can't find a job, and I owe more every day. Things are going from bad to worse.

ir(se) de parranda (v.) —To go on a drinking and carousing spree

ir de paso (v.) —To be in transit; to be just going through a place

ir(se) de pinta (v.) —*(Mex)* To play hooky ▪ *Es la tercera vez que esos niños se han ido de pinta este mes.* It's the third time those boys have played hooky this month.

ir disparado(a) (v.) —*(Mex)* To go in a great hurry (*lit.* to go like a shot) ▪ *Acabo de encontrarme con Lionel. Iba disparado.* I just ran into

Lionel. He was going like a bat out of hell.

ir hecho(a) la mocha (v.) —*(Mex)* (slang) To go like a streak

ir(la) librando (v.) —To make ends meet ▪ *No van muy bien las ventas, pero más o menos la vamos librando. Sales aren't too good, but we are more or less making ends meet.*

ir mandado(a) (v.) —*(Cuba, Chi)* (slang) To go lickety-split; to fly

ir(la) pasando (v.) —To make ends meet

ir volando (volado(a)) (v.) —To go in a great hurry, in a rush, in a flash (*lit.* to go flying)

itacate (n.) —*(Gua, Mex)* A supply of food, originally wrapped in a large cotton handkerchief, to take on a trip

(una) jalada (n.) —(slang) An exaggeration ▪ *Eso de que Cristóbal se iba a Acapulco con Leticia, es una jalada.* *What Cristobal said about going to Acapulco with Leticia is a lot of bull.*

jalar(se) (v.) —*(Col)* (slang) To get drunk ▪ *Jorge se jala cada vez que sale con Juan. Jorge gets drunk every time he goes out with Juan.*

jalar(le) las orejas a (alguien) (v.) —To scold (someone); to bawl (someone) out (*lit.* to pull (someone's) ears) ▪ *Mi hijo está portándose mal; tengo que jalarle las orejas. My kid is behaving badly. I'm going to have to scold him.*

jalar parejo (v.) —To play ball; to pull your weight ▪ *Mi primo me hace ayudarlo, y después él no me ayuda. No jala parejo. My cousin makes me help him, but he doesn't lift a finger when it comes to helping me. He doesn't pull his weight.*

jamonear(se) (v.) —*(Ven)* (slang) To embrace and kiss in public

jarana (n.) —*(Peru)* A lively party with lots of music, dancing and drinking ▪ *Estuvo muy buena la jarana del domingo. Sunday's party was lots of fun.*

jefa (jefecita) (n.) —*(Mex)* (slang) Mother

jefe (jefecito) (n.) —*(Mex)* (slang) Father

jeringar a (alguien) (v.) —To bother (someone) consistently; to bug (someone); to pester (*lit.* to pump a syringe) ▪ *Por última vez, ¡no te voy a prestar nada! Ya no estés jeringando. For the last time, I will not lend you any money! Stop bugging me.*

jorobar a (alguien) (v.) —To bother (someone) consistently; to bug (someone); to pester

jugar(sela) (v.) —To take a risk or a chance ▪ *Me la voy a jugar. Voy a pedirle aumento al jefe. I'm going to take the risk. I'll ask my boss for a salary increase.*

jugar con fuego (v.) —To play with fire; to skate on thin ice

justo a tiempo (adv.) —In the nick of time ▪ *Llegué a la reunión justo a tiempo. I got to the meeting in the nick of time.*

L

lambiscón (lambiscona) (n.) (adj.) —*(Mex)* Brownnoser; flatterer

lana (n.) —*(Mex)* Money; dough; bread (*lit.* wool)

lanzar de la casa a (alguien) (v.) —To evict (someone)

latir(le) (algo a alguien) (v.) —To have a hunch; to have a gut feeling; to feel (something) in your bones ▪ *Me late que no va a venir. I have a hunch that he is not coming. (He is not coming. I can feel it in my bones.)*

lavativa (n.) —1) An enema —2) *(Ven)* (slang) A pain in the neck (said of situations) ▪ *¡Qué lavativa! What a pain!*

levantar(se) con el pie izquierdo (v.) —To get up on the wrong side of the bed (*lit.* to get up with your left foot)

librar(la) (v.) —To be successful at something; to manage to do something (*lit.* to get around or over an obstacle, such as a hurdle) ▪ *Pensé que no íbamos a tener suficiente dinero para las colegiaturas, pero finalmente la libramos. I thought we wouldn't have enough money for the tuition, but in the end, we managed to scrape it together.*

(un) libre (n.) —A taxi (*lit.* a free one) ▪ *Tengo 10 minutos aquí y no pasa ni un libre. I've been standing here for ten minutes, and not a single cab has gone by.*

libre de polvo y paja (adv.) —Free of all charges

lisura (n.) —*(Peru)* Swear words or dirty language ▪ *No digas lisuras delante de las damas. Don't use bad language in front of the ladies.*

¡Lo dificulto! (v.) —*(Arg)* I doubt it!; I don't think so.

lucir(se) (v.) —1) To do (something) beautifully, usually to impress (someone); to do a great job of (something) ▪ *¡Qué hermoso pastel! ¡Te luciste! What a gorgeous cake! You outdid yourself!* —2) To do (something) bad; to make an impression by doing (something) negative ▪ *¿Cómo se te ocurrió traer a tu amigote a la comida de Lucina? ¡Te luciste! How could you bring your crummy pal to Lucina's lunch? You made a spectacle of yourself!*

lucir(le) el dinero (v.) —To be good at managing money ▪ *No sé cómo le hace. Gloria gana menos que yo y le luce más el dinero. I don't know how Gloria does it. She makes less than I do, but makes that money go farther.*

llamarada de petate (n.) —*(Mex)* A flash in the pan ▪ *Tus buenos propósitos nada más fueron llamarada de petate.* Your good intentions were nothing more than a flash in the pan.

llamar(le) al pan pan, y al vino vino (v.) —To call a spade a spade

¡Llégale! —*(Mex)* Have a go at it!

llegar a ser (v.) —To become something (over an extended period of time) ▪ *¿Crees que Alejandro realmente llegue a ser abogado?* Do you think Alejandro can really become a lawyer some day?

llegar(le) el agua a las narices (v.) —*(Ecu)* To be up to here; to be in hot water; to be at the breaking point

llegar(le) el agua al cuello (v.) —*(Mex)* To be up to here; to be in hot water; to be at the breaking point

llevar al baile a (alguien) (v.) —To trick (someone) (*lit.* to take someone to the dance) ▪ *No es Gucci. Me llevaron al baile.* It's not a Gucci. I've been had.

llevar(le) (X) años a (alguien) (v.) —To be (X) years older than (someone) ▪ *Le lleva ocho años a su esposa.* He is eight years older than his wife.

llevar(se) bien (mal) con (alguien) (v.) —To get along well (badly) with (someone) ▪ *Pedro y yo nos llevamos muy bien, pero me llevo mal con su hermano.* Pedro and I get along fine, but I don't get along with his brother.

llevar(se) el tren a (alguien) (v.) —(slang) To be or get fed up ▪ *¡Me lleva el tren!* Hell!

llevar(le) la contra a (alguien) (v.) —To be contrary ▪ *Siempre me lleva la contra.* He's always against everything I say or do.

llevar(se) la palma (v.) —To take the prize for (something) bad ▪ *Llegó medio borracho a la fiesta de su novia. ¡Se llevó la palma!* He arrived at his girlfriend's party half-plastered. That really takes the cake!

llover a cántaros (v.) —To rain cats and dogs

llover(le) insultos (golpes) a (alguien) (v.) —To be pelted with insults (blows) ▪ *Cuando tomó el micrófono, le llovieron insultos.* When he went to the microphone, he was pelted with insults.

llover sobre mojado (v.) —One thing after another; it doesn't rain, but it pours (*lit.* to rain on wet ground) ▪ *El año pasado tuve hepatitis, y ahora salmonelosis. ¡Me está lloviendo sobre mojado!* Last year it was hepatitis and now I've got salmonellosis. What kind of lousy luck is that?

M

macanudo(a) (adj.) —*(Arg)* (slang) Super; marvelous; terrific; cool

maceta (n.) —*(Mex)* (slang) Head (*lit.* flowerpot)

macho(a) (n.) (adj.) —1) *(CR)* A blond male foreigner; blond; a fair-complexioned female —2) *(Mex)* A he-man —3) *(Mex)* courageous ▪ *José es muy macho, no quiso anestesia para que lo cosieran. Jose is really brave. He refused anesthesia when the doctor was sewing him up.*

machucar (v.) —1) *(Peru)* (slang) To beat (someone) up —2) *(Mex)* To mash (cooking) or squash (e.g., a thumb)

maje (n.) —*(Mex)* (slang) A not very bright person

mal habido(a) (adj.) —Ill-gotten ▪ *Su fortuna es mal habida. His fortune is ill-gotten.*

mala leche (n.) —Malice

mala pata (n.) —Bad luck

maliciar (v.) —To have a bad hunch about (something); to smell (something) fishy ▪ *Estoy maliciando que todo fue una jugarreta de tus socios. I have a feeling that the whole thing was a trick planned by your partners.*

malorear a (alguien) (v.) —(slang) To bother people; to pick on (someone) ▪ *Se la pasa maloreando a sus amigos. He's always picking on his friends.*

mamar(se) (v.) —*(Arg)* (slang) To get drunk

mamar gallo (v.) —*(Col, Ven)* (slang) To fool around; to horse around

mandamás (n.) —(The, a) big shot

mandar(se) (v.) —(slang) To go too far; to get carried away ▪ *Una cosa es ser sincero y otra ser grosero con tu mamá. ¡Te mandaste! It's one thing to be frank with your mother and another to be rude. You went too far.*

mandar al cuerno a (alguien) (v.) —To send (someone) to hell; to tell (someone) to jump in the lake (*lit.* to send someone to the horn) ▪ *No le vayas a prestar otra vez el coche a tu cuñada. ¡Mándala al cuerno! Don't lend your sister-in-law the car again. Send her to hell!*

mandar al chorizo a (alguien) (v.) —*(Gua)* To send (someone) to hell; to tell (someone) to jump in the lake

mandar por un tubo a (alguien) (v.) —(slang) To send (someone) to hell; to tell (someone) to jump in the lake (*lit.* to send someone down a pipe) ▪ *Le pedí un aumento y me mandó por un tubo. I asked for a raise and he sent me to hell.*

¿Mande? (v.) —Yes? (a reply when called by name) (*lit.* Command me!, an expression leftover from other times)

manga de (algo) (n.) —*(Arg)* (slang) A lot of something ▪ *¡Mira esa manga de vagos! Look at that bunch of loiterers.*

mangonear a (alguien) (v.) —To manipulate (someone); to boss (someone) around; to push (someone) around ▪ *Cuando eres el hermano menor, siempre te mangonean. When you're the younger brother, you always get used and pushed around.*

más asustado que una cucaracha (adv.) —*(Col)* Really scared; scared out of your wits ▪ *La pobre de Gina tiene que presentar el examen y está más asustada que una cucaracha. Poor Gina has to take the test, and she's scared silly.*

matar los ojos (v.) —*(Ven)* (slang) To look daggers at (someone) ▪ *Ese muchacho me está matando los ojos. That guy is looking daggers at me.*

matar un burro a pellizcos (v.) *(Col, Cuba, Ecu)* —Something that is very difficult to achieve; to fly to the moon (*lit.* to pinch a donkey to death) ▪ *Eso es más difícil que matar un burro a pellizcos. That just can't be done.*

mear(se) fuera de la bacinica (v.) —To miss the point (*lit.* to miss the pot when you're peeing) ▪ *Entendiste mal lo que te dijo Alfonso. Te estás meando fuera de la bacinica. You misunderstood what Alfonso said. You've got it all wrong.*

media naranja (n.) —Better half ▪ *Por fin Paco encontró su media naranja. Paco finally found his better half.*

menear el bote (v.) —*(Mex)* (slang) To dance (*lit.* to wiggle your bucket)

¡Menos mal! —Thank goodness! ▪ *Acabábamos de entrar y se soltó lloviendo. ¡Menos mal! We made it inside before it started pouring. Thank goodness! ¡Menos mal que todo salió bien! Thank goodness everything turned out well!*

menso(a) (n.) (adj.) —Stupid; a stupid person

meter(se) con (alguien) (v.) —1) To mess with (someone or something); to look for trouble with (someone) ▪ *¡No te metas conmigo! Don't mess with me!* —2) To get involved with (someone)

meter (la) (su) cuchara (v.) —To butt in; to put in your two cents worth (*lit.* to stick in your spoon) ▪ *Estoy hablando con Fernando. Por favor no metas tu cuchara. I'm talking to Fernando. Please don't butt in.*

meter(se) en camisa de once varas (v.) —To bite off more than you can chew (*lit.* to wear a shirt eleven "varas" long—one "vara"= 83.5

cm) ▪ *Si te asocias con Tomás, vas a meterte en camisa de once varas.* *If you go into business with Tomás, you'll be biting off more than you can chew.*

meter en cintura (v.) —To bring an unruly child or person under control ▪ *El profesor no tiene energía para meter a sus alumnos en cintura.* *The professor doesn't have the energy to get tough with his students.*

meter(se) en la grande (v.) —*(Col)* To get into hot water ▪ *¿Cómo se te ocurre provocar a Roberto? Ya te metiste en la grande.* *What do you think you're doing by offending Roberto? Now you're really in hot water.*

meter la mano al fuego por (alguien) (v.) —To vouch for (someone) ▪ *Carmen no es ninguna mentirosa. Meto la mano al fuego por ella.* *Carmen is not a liar. I'll vouch for her.*

meter(le) mano a (algo) (v.) —To monkey with (something) ▪ *Ya veo el problema. Alguien le metió mano al carburador.* *Now I see the problem. Someone monkeyed with the carburetor.*

meter(le) mano a (alguien) (v.) —To fondle (someone's) private parts

meter(le) vales a la caja (v.) —*(Ven)* To have sex before marriage (*lit.* to put vouchers in the till) ▪ *Esos dos ya le están metiendo vales a la caja y la boda es hasta mayo.* *Those two are having sex and they're not even getting married until May.*

mientras que son peras o son manzanas ... —Until this can be cleared up or figured out ... ▪ *No nos mandaron el desglose de la factura, pero mientras que son peras o son manzanas, hay que pagarla.* *They didn't provide a breakdown of the invoice, but in the meantime, it has to be paid.*

mirar de arriba abajo a (alguien) (v.) —To give (someone) the once-over

mirar feo a (alguien) (v.) —(slang) To look daggers at (someone)

misturar a (alguien) (v.) —*(Arg)* (slang) To confuse (someone)

mitote (n.) —(slang) A big stink

mochar(se) (v.) —1) *(Mex)* (slang) To cut off ▪ *El trabajador se mochó un dedo con la máquina.* *The worker cut off his finger with the machine.* —2) To go jump in the lake ▪ *Ya nos tienes hartos, ¡móchate!* *We are sick and tired of you. Beat it!* —3) To share (something) with (someone) ▪ *¡Móchate con unas cheves!* *Share some beers with us!*

mocho(a) (n.) (adj.) —*(Mex)* (slang) A very pious Catholic (derogatory) ▪ *Julián no toma alcohol, ni come carne los viernes. Es muy mocho.* *Julian doesn't drink alcohol and he eats no meat on Fridays. He's a fanatic Catholic.*

mojigato(a) (n.) (adj.) —A very pious Catholic (derogatory)

molón (molona) (n.) (adj.) —*(Mex)* (slang) (Someone) who is a pain in the neck

(la) momiza (n.) —*(Mex)* (slang) Collective noun referring to adult, old people; senior citizens (from **momia**: mummy) ▪ *Aquí no... aquí se sienta la pura momiza. Not here... all the old fogies sit here.*

montar(se) en su macho (v.) —To get stubborn ▪ *Traté de razonar con él, pero se montó en su macho y no quiso escucharme.* I tried to reason with him, but he got stubborn and wouldn't listen.

morder(se) la lengua (v.) —To criticize (someone) for a defect from which you also suffer ▪ *No digas eso, porque te muerdes la lengua.* People who live in glass houses shouldn't throw stones.

morir(se) por (alguien o algo) (v.) —To die for (someone or something) ▪ *Hace calor. Me muero por un refresco. It's so awfully hot! I'm dying for a cool drink!*

mota (n.) —(slang) Marijuana

motoso (n.) —*(Col)* (slang) A nap

mover cielo, mar y tierra (v.) —To bend over backwards; to go to great lengths; to go to the ends of the earth to get (something) done ▪ *¡Qué lindo José Antonio! Movió cielo, mar y tierra para conseguirme el departamento que quería. José Antonio is a dear! He went to great lengths to get me the apartment I wanted.*

mover el bote (v.) —(slang) To dance (*lit.* to move your can)

mover(le) el tapete a (alguien) (v.) —To plot against (someone) (*lit.* to move the rug under someone's feet)

mover influencias (v.) —To pull strings

mover palancas (v.) —To pull strings (*lit.* to move levers)

(una) mugre (n.) —(slang) (something) really worthless or undesirable ▪ *Este radio es una mugre. This radio is a piece of crap.*

nacer(le) (v.) —Said when (something) comes naturally (or, in the negative, when it goes against the grain) ▪ *Le da regalos a todo el mundo en Navidad porque le nace.* He gives everyone gifts at Christmas just because he feels like it. *No me pidas que bese a la Tía Rosa. No me nace.* Don't ask me to kiss Aunt Rose. It goes against the grain.

naco(a) (n.) (adj.) —*(Mex)* (slang) A person who is crass, vulgar, gross, uneducated, ignorant, rude, etc.

nave (n.) —*(Arg, Col, Gua, Mex)* (slang) A car

(la) neta (n.) —*(Mex)* (slang) The truth ▪ *La neta, no te entiendo.* To tell you the truth, I don't get what you are talking about.

¡Ni a tiros! (adv.) —Not for love or money; No way! ▪ *Esos no ganan el juego ni a tiros.* There's no way those guys are going to win the game.

¡Ni con chochos! (adv.) —*(Mex)* No way!

¡Ni de chiste! (adv.) —It's out of the question!; Not on your life! ▪ *Alberto quiere que me tire con él en paracaídas. ¡Ni de chiste!* Alberto wants me to parachute with him. Not on your life!

¡Ni en cuenta! (adv.) —Didn't notice; it is not important (from **no tomar en cuenta**: to not take into consideration)

ni fu ni fa (adj.) —Neither good nor bad ▪ *La sopa estuvo exquisita, pero las enchiladas, ni fu ni fa.* The soup was divine, but the enchiladas were just so-so.

¡Ni idea! (adv.) —It beats me! ▪ *De lo que me preguntaste… ¡Ni idea!* As for your question… it beats me!

¡Ni jota! (adv.) —Zero; zilch; nothing ▪ *Raúl no habla ni jota de inglés.* Raul speaks no English at all.

¡Ni loco(a)! (adv.) —I'd be crazy to do that!

¡Ni mandado a hacer! (adv.) —Just perfect! ▪ *¡Mira cómo me quedan tus pantalones! ¡Ni mandados a hacer!* Look how your pants fit me! Just perfect!

Ni me va ni me viene. —I don't care.; It's all the same to me.

¡Ni modo(s)! —It can't be helped!; There's nothing we can do about that!; That's the way the ball bounces!; That's too bad!; That's bad luck!

ni papa (adv.) —Nothing at all ▪ *No sé ni papa de alemán.* I don't know a word of German.

ni por todo el oro del mundo (adv.) —Not for love or money

ni quería —I didn't want that anyway (sour grapes)

ningunear a (alguien) (v.) —(slang) To ignore or pay no attention to (someone) (from **ninguno**: none or no one)

no abundar(le) (v.) —*(ES)* To have very little of something ■ *A tu papá no le abunda el dinero. Your dad doesn't have much money.*

no dar golpe (v.) —To be perpetually out of a job ■ *Jorge no da golpe. Siempre va a ser un inútil. Jorge is always out of a job. He's going to be useless all his life.*

no dar paso sin guarache (sin linterna) (v.) —*(Mex)* (slang) To do nothing unless there is some kind of advantage to be had ■ *No esperes que Quique te ayude. No da paso sin guarache. Don't expect Quique to help you. He doesn't do anything unless there is something in it for him.*

no dar pie con bola (v.) —To make no headway; to be completely inept; to do everything wrong ■ *En dominó es muy bueno, pero en ajedrez no da pie con bola. He's very good at dominoes, but he's lousy at chess.*

no dar una (v.) —To make no headway at all; to be completely inept; to do everything wrong ■ *Francisco no da una. Creo que está crudo. Francisco can't get anything right. I think he has a hangover.*

no dejar(se) (v.) —To not let people take advantage of you ■ *Si te echa bronca, aunque esté grandulón, ¡no te dejes! If he picks a fight, don't let him push you around, even if he's bigger than you.*

no haber para cuándo (v.) —To show no signs of happening or being ready yet; to take ages ■ *Llevo dos semanas esperando cita con el Gerente y no hay para cuándo. I've been waiting for an appointment with the manager for two weeks, and there's no sign of it happening.*

no hacer(la) (v.) —*(Mex)* (slang) To fail to qualify or be up to par (*lit.* to not make it) ■ *¡Está horrible!; pintando no la haces. That picture is ghastly. You're no good as a painter.*

¡No hay de qué! (¡De nada!) —You're welcome.

no hay moros en la costa —The coast is clear ■ *Puedes venir, mi amor, ahorita no hay moros en la costa. You can come, dear. The coast is clear.*

No hay pero que valga. —No buts. ■ *Dijiste que hoy iban a estar listos los dibujos. ¡No hay pero que valga! You said the drawings were going to be ready today. No buts!*

no lucir(le) el dinero (v.) —To be bad at managing money ■ *Por más que gane, no le luce. No matter how much he makes, it just disappears.*

no llegar(le) ni a los talones a (alguien) (v.) —To be nothing compared to (someone); not to hold a candle to (someone)

no llegar(le) ni al tobillo a (alguien) (v.) —To be nothing compared to (someone); not to hold a candle to (someone)

no medir(se) (v.) —1) To go overboard; to do a really extraordinary job of (something) ▪ *Luis se puso muy grosero; no se midió.* Luis got really rude. He went too far. —2) To stop at nothing ▪ *Su casa nueva está increíble. No se midieron.* Their new house is unbelievable. They stopped at nothing.

no poder con el paquete (v.) —Not to be able to cope with (something) ▪ *Acepté llevar la contabilidad de la empresa, pero ahora me doy cuenta de que no puedo con el paquete.* I agreed to handle the company's accounting, but now I realize I can't cope with it.

no poder ver ni en pintura a (alguien) (v.) —To dislike (someone) thoroughly; not to be able to stand the sight of (someone) (*lit.* to hate seeing someone even in a picture) ▪ *El infeliz de Ernesto me ha hecho tantos chanchullos, que no lo puedo ver ni en pintura.* Ernesto has screwed me so many times that I can't stand the sight of him.

no romper un plato (v.) —To seem innocuous; to appear incapable of doing anything wrong (*lit.* to be incapable of breaking a plate) ▪ *¿Quién diría que Luis le pegó a Rafael? Parece que no rompe un plato.* Who would have thought that Luis would sock Rafael in the puss? He looks so sweet and innocent!

no saber ni a jícama (v.) —*(Mex)* Expression to describe (something) insipid or unchallenging ▪ *Finalmente jugué contra el gran profesional de tenis. No me supo ni a jícama.* I finally got to play against the great tennis pro. He didn't put up any kind of a fight.

no sacar pelo sin sangre (v.) —*(CR)* To do nothing unless there is some kind of advantage to be had ▪ *Carlos no saca pelo sin sangre.* Carlos doesn't do anything unless there's something in it for him.

¡No se te ocurra hacer (algo)! —For heaven's sake, don't … ▪ *¡No se te ocurra mascar chicle en la iglesia!* For heaven's sake don't chew gum in church!

no ser para tanto (v.) —To be less of a big deal than (someone) makes it out to be ▪ *Se enojó porque llegué un poco tarde. No es para tanto.* He got mad 'cause I was a little late. It's not that big of a deal.

no servir ni para loco (v.) —*(CR)* To be entirely useless (*lit.* to be useless, even as a lunatic) ▪ *Tu amigo es un inútil. ¡No sirve ni para loco!* That guy is totally useless. Good for absolutely nothing!

no soltar ni un quinto (v.) —To be stingy; to be a tightwad (*lit.* to not let go of even a nickel)

no soltar prenda (v.) —To be very discreet; to keep a secret; (not) to let the cat out of the bag

¡No son enchiladas! —*(Mex)* It's not that easy! (*lit.* It's not like making enchiladas!) ▪ *¿Quieres que haga la afinación en una hora? ¡No son enchiladas! You want me to do a tune-up in one hour? It's not that easy, you know!*

¡No te acalambres! —*(Mex)* (slang) Don't get all upset! (*lit.* Don't get a cramp!)

¡No te aceleres! —Hold your horses!

¡No te hagas! —(slang) Don't play dumb!

¡No te pases! —Don't overstep yourself!; Don't get smart!; Don't try to put one over on me! ▪ *Es mi hermana. No te pases. She's my sister. Don't try anything stupid with her.*

no tener caso (v.) —To be pointless; not to be worth it (*lit.* to have no case) ▪ *No tiene caso insistir, es muy necio. There's no point in insisting. He's very stubborn.*

no tener cerebro ni para un derrame (v.) —*(CR)* To be an idiot; be very stupid (*lit.* not to have enough brains to have a stroke)

no tener dos dedos de frente (v.) —To be an idiot; be very stupid (*lit.* to have a forehead that measures less than two fingers from eyebrows to hairline) ▪ *No le pidas a ese pobre que organice el departamento. No tiene dos dedos de frente. Don't expect that poor guy to organize the department. He's really dumb.*

no tener nombre (v.) —To be unspeakable ▪ *Lo que hiciste no tiene nombre. What you did is unspeakable!*

no tener para cuándo (v.) —To show no signs of happening

no tener pelos en la lengua (v.) —To be very outspoken (*lit.* to have no hairs on your tongue) ▪ *Nicolás no se anda con rodeos. No tiene pelos en la lengua. Nicolás doesn't beat around the bush. He really tells it like it is.*

¡No tenga pena! —*(Gua)* Don't worry!

No todo es miel sobre hojuelas. —It's not all fun and games.

no ver(le) ni el polvo a (alguien) (v.) —Said when (someone) leaves in an enormous hurry (*lit.* to not even see the dust kicked up in a hurried departure) ▪ *En cuanto llegó la policía, Juan desapareció. No le vimos ni el polvo. As soon as the police arrived, Juan vanished.*

ñapa (n.) —*(Bol, Peru)* Lagniappe; bonus; gratuity; baker's dozen

orinar(se) fuera de la bacinica (v.) —To miss the point (*lit.* to miss the pot when you're peeing) ▪ *Entendiste mal lo que te dijo Alfonso. Te estás orinando fuera de la bacinica. You misunderstood what Alfonso said. You've got it all wrong.*

¡Pa' su mecha! —*(Mex)* (slang) Holy cow!

paco (n.) —*(Ecu)* (slang) Policeman

pachocha (n.) —1) *(Peru)* (slang) Parsimony; frugality ▪ *Va caminando con una gran pachocha.* She walks with great economy of movement. —2) *(Mex)* Money ▪ *Me encontré una billetera llena de pachocha.* I found a wallet with a lot of money.

pachochín (n.) —*(Peru)* (slang) A dumb person ▪ *No lo parece, pero es un pachochín.* He doesn't look it, but he's not all that bright.

pachuco(a) (n.) —*(CR)* lowlife; ruffian

pagar el pato (v.) —To be made the scapegoat; to be blamed (or take the blame) for (someone) else's mistake or wrongdoing (*lit.* to pay for the dead duck)

pagar los platos rotos (v.) —To be made the scapegoat; to be blamed (or take the blame) for (someone) else's mistake or wrongdoing (*lit.* to pay for the broken dishes)

pagar una fortuna (v.) —To pay through the nose

pajuela (n.) —*(Bol)* A match

palito trinador (n.) —*(Peru)* (slang) A guitar

paluchear (v.) —*(Cuba)* (slang) To pretend to be (something) you're not ▪ *A Carlos le gusta paluchear.* Carlos is always posturing as something he really isn't.

pando(a) (n.) (adj.) *(Bol)* (slang) —1) Shallow —2) hunchback

panear (v.) —*(Bol)* (slang) To show off

pantallero(a) (n.) (adj.) —*(Arg, Ven, Col)* (slang) A loudmouth show-off

papa pelada (n.) —*(Ven)* (slang) A piece of cake; (something) that is very easy

papaya (n.) —1) Fruit —2) (vulgar) Feminine private parts

papear (v.) —*(Peru)* To stuff yourself ▪ *Papeamos a lo bárbaro.* We really stuffed ourselves!

papiar (v.) —*(Col)* (slang) To win by making the other person look ridiculous

para aventar para arriba (adv.) —More than you can shake a stick at ▪ *Tiene juguetes para aventar para arriba.* He's got more toys than you can shake a stick at.

---

para colmo (adv.) —To make things worse; to top things off ■ *Este mes perdí el empleo y estuve una semana en el hospital.Y para colmo, ¡ayer me robaron el coche!* This month I lost my job and was in the hospital for a week. And to make matters worse, my car was stolen yesterday!

para eso me pinto solo(a) (adv.) —That's what I'm really good at (*lit.* I paint myself without any help) ■ *Para cocinar me pinto solo.* I am an absolutely marvelous cook.

¡Para nada! —Not at all!; No way! ■ *Elena le dijo a su hermana que soy de ascendencia alemana. ¡Para nada!* Elena told her sister that my forebears are German. Not at all!

para quitar el hipo (adj.) —Very impressive; astonishing (*lit.* enough to cure the hiccups) ■ *¡Gabriela se compró en París unos vestidos para quitar el hipo!* Gabriela bought some absolutely stunning dresses in Paris.

parar(se) de pestañas (v.) —To hit the ceiling; to raise a terrible fuss; to make a fuss; to make a stink about (something) (*lit.* to stand on your eyelashes) ■ *Cuando le dijeron a Gaby que Jorge la engaña, se paró de pestañas.* You should have seen Gaby when they told her Jorge is being unfaithful! She had a fit!

pargo (n.) —1) A type of fish —2) *(Ven)* (slang) A homosexual

parir borugos (v.) —*(Col)* (slang) To be in a bind; to go through a difficult situation ■ *¿De dónde voy a sacar tanto dinero en una semana? ¡Me están poniendo a parir borugos!* Where am I expected to get all that money in only a week? Now I'm really in a bind!

parir chayotes (v.) —*(Mex)* (slang) To be in a bind; to go through a difficult situation (*lit.* to give birth to **chayotes** (a large vegetable covered with thornlike spines)) ■ *La preparación de este informe me puso a parir chayotes.* Writing this report was an excruciating process.

parquear (v.) —*(CR)* To park

parqueo (n.) —*(CR)* Parking lot

pasar(se) de maraca (v.) —*(Ven)* (slang) To go too far; to try to pull off a fast one ■ *No te pases de maraca conmigo.* Don't get smart with me!

pasar(sele) la mano a (alguien) (v.) —(slang) To go too far ■ *Eloísa está en su cuarto llora que llora. ¡Ahora sí se te pasó la mano!* Eloisa is in her room crying her eyes out.You really went too far this time!

pasar la pena negra (v.) —To have a terrible time of something

pasar(se) la preventiva (pasar(se) la luz amarilla) (v.) —To drive through a yellow light

pasar(sele) las cucharadas a (alguien) (v.) —To have one too many (alcohol) (*lit.* to have too many spoonfuls)

pasar las de Caín (v.) —To go through hell (*lit.* to experience what Cain went through)

pasar una corta a (alguien) (v.) —*(Mex)* (slang) To bribe; to fork out some dough; to grease (someone's) hand

pase lo que pase (adv.) —Come hell or high water

patinar(le) el coco (v.) —(slang) To be nuts ▪ *El maestro dice que va a inventar una máquina de movimiento perpetuo. ¡Le patina el coco!* The teacher says he's going to invent a perpetual motion machine. He's really nuts!

patojo(a) —1) (n.) *(Gua)* (slang) A boy or girl ▪ *Se enamoró de esa patoja.* He fell in love with that girl. —2) (adj.) *(Ecu)* Lame (people and animals); rickety (furniture) ▪ *La silla está patoja.* That chair is rickety.

pavada (n.) —*(Arg)* (slang) Silliness

pedir(le) peras al olmo (v.) —To ask the impossible (*lit.* to expect an elm to bear pears) ▪ *¿Tú crees que Alejandra va a estar lista en 20 minutos? No le pidas peras al olmo.* You think Alejandra will be ready in 20 minutes? You're asking the impossible.

pegar con tubo (v.) —(slang) To be very successful or very impressive (*lit.* to wham with a pipe)

pegar de gritos (v.) —To yell; to let out a series of screams

pegar(sele) las sábanas a (alguien) (v.) —To oversleep (*lit.* to have the sheets stick to someone) ▪ *¡Mira a qué horas llegas! ¿Se te pegaron las sábanas?* Look what time you're getting here! Did you oversleep?

pegar(le) un grito a (alguien) (v.) —To yell; to let (someone) know; to give (someone) a yell or a phone call ▪ *Cuando esté listo el informe, pégame un grito.* Let me know (Give me a yell) when the report is ready.

pegar(le) un susto a (alguien) (v.) —To scare or startle (someone) ▪ *¡Me pegaste un susto!* You scared me!

peladeces (n.) —*(Mex)* Bad language; swear words ▪ *No digas peladeces ante las damas.* Don't use that kind of language in front of the ladies.

pelagatos (n.) —A worthless person (*lit.* a cat skinner) ▪ *Esos pelagatos deberían encontrar algo que hacer.* Those dudes should find something to do with themselves.

pelar gajo (v.) —*(Ven)* (slang) To make a mistake

pelar la pava (v.) —*(Arg, Peru, Mex)* (slang) To chatter with your girlfriend

pelar rata (v.) —*(Gua)* (slang) To make a mistake ▪ *Pelaste rata con la*

respuesta. *Your answer was way off base.*

pensionar (v.) —*(Ecu)* (slang) To bother

peor-es-nada (n.) —A colloquial, humorous and mocking term used to describe a girlfriend or boyfriend (*lit.* better than nothing) ▪ *Anoche hubo una cena y estuvo Micaela con su peor-es-nada. There was a dinner party last night, and Micaela was there with that wishy-washy, useless boyfriend of hers.*

perder los estribos (v.) —To fly off the handle; to lose control of yourself (*lit.* to lose your stirrups)

pesar peor que un mal matrimonio (v.) —*(CR)* To weigh a ton (*lit.* to weigh worse than a bad marriage)

pescar a (alguien) (v.) —*(Arg)* To catch (someone) doing something wrong

pescar(las) al vuelo (v.) —(slang) To be as bright as a new penny, as sharp as a knife (*lit.* to catch them in the air or in flight) ▪ *No es fácil engañar a Ricardo. Las pesca al vuelo. It's not easy to fool Ricardo. He's a really sharp guy.*

pescar una enfermedad (v.) —To catch an illness

petatear(se) (v.) —*(Mex)* (slang) To kick the bucket (*lit.* to lie or fall on the **petate** (straw sleeping mat)) ▪ *Nadie se imaginó que la señora iba a petatearse en plena fiesta. No one had any idea that lady was going to kick the bucket in the middle of the party.*

pez gordo (n.) —Fat cat (*lit.* fat fish) ▪ *Nunca encarcelan a los peces gordos. The fat cats never get thrown in jail.*

pibe (n.) —*(Arg)* (slang) Boy

picar(se) (v.) —1) (slang) To get hooked or caught up with something that may not have been particularly interesting at the outset ▪ *Ya me piqué con el juego. Now I'm hooked on this game.* —2) *(Ecu)* To get drunk ▪ *En la fiesta de anoche nos picamos más de la cuenta. We drank too much at last night's party.*

picar mucho (v.) —*(Mex)* To be very spicy; to be very hot (food)

pichicato(a) —1) (adj.) *(Mex)* (slang) Stingy —2) (n.) Miser

pichirre (adj.) —*(Ven)* (slang) Stingy

piña (n.) (adj.) —*(Ven)* (slang) A pain in the neck ▪ *Estela es una piña. Estela is a pain in the neck.*

pisar (v.) —1) To step on; to tread; to set foot —2) *(Gua, Mex)* (vulgar) To copulate (originally applied to birds)

plata (n.) —*(CR, Arg, Uru, Chi)* Money

pocho(a) (n.) —1) *(CR)* A dark-complexioned person —2) *(Mex)* A Mexican born in Texas or on the other side of the Mexico/United States border and whose culture is neither entirely Mexican nor entirely American

poder(le) mucho a (alguien) (v.) —*(Mex)* To be greatly saddened or depressed by (something) ▪ *Le pudo mucho la muerte de su mamá. The death of his mother really got him down.*

polo (n.) —*(CR)* (slang) Lowlife; ruffian

pololear (v.) —*(Bol)* (slang) To compliment

polla (n.) —*(Ecu)* A crib sheet; secret notes to copy from in a test

pompas (pompis) (n.) —*(Mex)* (slang) Derrière; buns

poner a (alguien o algo) por las nubes (los cielos) (v.) —To praise (someone or something) to the skies ▪ *David estaba hablando de música mexicana. Puso a Carlos Chávez por los cielos. David was talking about Mexican music, and he praised Carlos Chavez to the skies.*

poner(se) a tono con (alguien) (v.) —To act the same way as (someone else) ▪ *Olvídate de lo que dijo. No te pongas a tono con ese tonto. Forget what he said. Don't stoop to the same level as that idiot.*

poner(se) abusado(a) (v.) —*(Mex)* (slang) To get or to be on the alert for an opportunity or eventuality ▪ *En esta calle hay mucho carterista. ¡Pónte abusado! There are a lot of pickpockets on this street. Be careful!*

poner cara de palo (v.) —To make a poker face (*lit.* to make a wooden face)

poner cara larga (v.) —To look upset, sulky or down in the mouth (*lit.* to make a long face)

poner(se) color de hormiga (v.) —*(ES, Mex)* To become very difficult (situations) ▪ *Por tu culpa, la cosa se puso color de hormiga. The situation got very difficult, thanks to you.*

poner como lazo de cochino a (alguien) (v.) —*(Mex)* To jump down (someone's) throat (*lit.* to make someone look like a pig's ribbon) ▪ *Al cuate ése lo pusieron como lazo de cochino. That guy was thoroughly bawled out.*

poner como palo de gallinero a (alguien) (v.) —To jump down (someone's) throat (*lit.* to make someone look like a roosting stick in a chicken coop)

poner(se) de malas (v.) —To get in a bad mood ▪ *Mi jefe ya se puso* *de malas.* *My boss has got into a foul mood.*

poner de malas a (alguien) (v.) —To get (someone) into a bad mood ▪ *Mi hermano me puso de malas. My brother got me into a foul mood.*

poner de patitas en la calle a (alguien) (v.) —To throw (someone) out on their ear; to boot (someone) out ▪ *En vez de aumentarle el sueldo, lo pusieron de patitas en la calle. Instead of giving him a raise, they kicked him out!*

poner el dedo (v.) —*(ES)* To point out

poner el dedo en la llaga (v.) —To touch a sore spot (*lit.* to put your finger on the sore)

poner el grito en el cielo (v.) —To hit the ceiling; to make a big fuss; to make a stink (*lit.* to put the scream in the sky) ▪ *Sofía puso el grito en el cielo porque fue la única que no ascendieron. Sofía made an awful stink because she was the only one that wasn't promoted.*

poner(se) en ridículo (v.) —To make a fool of yourself; to make (someone) look bad ▪ *¡Qué pena! Por hablar tonterías, te pusiste en ridículo. How embarrassing! You made a fool of yourself talking nonsense.*

poner(se) enérgico(a) (v.) —To become very strict and stern in imposing a rule or setting things right ▪ *Hay que apegarnos a las políticas. El nuevo gerente se está poniendo muy enérgico. We have to stick to the policies. The new manager is getting very strict.*

poner(sele) la carne de gallina (v.) —To give (someone) the creeps (*lit.* to give someone chicken skin)

poner(se) las pilas (v.) —*(Ven)* To perk up and get on the ball (*lit.* to put in your batteries)

poner(le) los cuernos a (alguien) (v.) —*(Mex)* To be unfaithful to (someone); to make a cuckold of (someone) (*lit.* to put horns on someone) ▪ *Luis le pone los cuernos a su mujer. Luis is not faithful to his wife. (Luis has affairs with other women.)*

poner(le) los pelos de punta a (alguien) (v.) —To give (someone) the creeps (*lit.* to make someone's hair stand up on end) ▪ *Había una araña en la puerta que me puso los pelos de punta. There was a spider on the door that made my hair stand up on end.*

poner peros (v.) —To make objections ▪ *Tienes que acabar tu tarea. No pongas peros. You have to finish your homework. No buts.*

poner(se) sus moños (v.) —To get snotty about something

poner(le) un cuatro a (alguien) (v.) —To set a trap for (someone)

- **La policía le está poniendo un cuatro.** *The police are laying a trap for him.*

poner(se) una soba (v.) —To tire yourself out; to knock yourself out

poner(le) zancadilla a (alguien) (v.) —*(CR)* To screw (someone); to do (someone) a bad deed (*lit.* to kick someone in the shins) ▪ *Alberto me puso zancadilla enfrente de Laura.* *Alberto let me have it, right in front of Laura.*

por debajo del agua (adv.) —Under the table (*lit.* under the water)

por estos rumbos (adv.) —In this neck of the woods ▪ *¿Qué te trae por estos rumbos?* *What brings you to this neck of the woods?*

por la buena (adv.) —Nicely; without having to be forced ▪ *Por la buena les doy lo que quieran.* *If you ask nicely, I'll give you anything you want.*

por la mala (adv.) —Only when forced (punished) ▪ *Jorge es llevado de por la mala.* *You can only get Jorge to do things by threatening him.*

por las (re)cochinas dudas (adv.) —*(Mex)* Just in case ▪ *Por las cochinas dudas, voy a mandar investigar a ese muchacho.* *I'm going to have that boy investigated, just in case.*

por lo pronto (adv.) —In the meantime; until we see what happens next ▪ *Por lo pronto viviré en un hotel.* *For the time being, I'll live in a hotel.*

por si acaso (adv.) —Just in case

por si fuera poco (adv.) —To add insult to injury ▪ *Me insultó delante de mis amigos, y por si fuera poco, se fue sin pagar la cuenta.* *He insulted me in front of my friends. And to add insult to injury, he went off without paying the bill!*

por si las moscas (adv.) —Just in case

por todos los rincones (adv.) —In every nook and cranny

por tuberías (adv.) —*(Cuba)* (slang) In large quantities ▪ *Hubo ron por tuberías.* *There was rum running in the gutters.*

por un pelito (adv.) —By very little (*lit.* by a little hair) ▪ *No le pegaste a ese camión por un pelito.* *You missed that bus by a second.*

por un pelo de rana (adv.) —By very little (*lit.* by a frog's hair)

porotos verdes (n.) —*(Arg, Chi)* String beans

prender(sele) el foco a (alguien) (v.) —1) To get a bright idea (*lit.* to have your lightbulb light up) ▪ *Ya estaba acostado cuando se me prendió el foco.* *I was in bed when I got a bright idea.* —2) To finally understand or remember something; to have everything fall into place

prestar(se) a muchas interpretaciones (v.) —To be open to many interpretations

prometer(le) el oro y el moro a (alguien) (v.) —To promise (someone) the Earth ▪ *Me prometió el oro y el moro, pero preferí quedarme soltera. He offered me the Earth, but I preferred to stay single.*

prometer(le) la luna y las estrellas a (alguien) (v.) —To promise (someone) the moon and stars

provocar un entrevero (v.) —*(Arg)* To cause confusion, disorder

¡Pura vida! —*(CR)* Fabulous! ▪ *¿Cómo estás? ¡Pura vida! ¿Cómo estuvo la fiesta? ¡Pura vida! How are you? Terrific! How was the party? Marvelous!*

Q

¡Qué barbaridad! —Oh, no!; How awful!; How incredible!; What a disaster!; Imagine that!; Good God!

¡Qué bárbaro(a)! —Good Lord!; Heavens!; Crikey! (said in admiration of something amazingly good or awful that someone has done) ▪ *¡Qué bárbaro! ¡Hizo 200 lagartijas! Wow! He did 200 pushups!*

¡Qué camello! —*(Col)* (slang) That's not going to be easy!

¡Qué concha! —(slang) What nerve! ▪ *Me dejó pagar toda la cuenta, ¡qué concha! He let me pay the entire bill! What nerve!!*

¡Qué churro! —*(Mex)* (slang) What good luck!

¡Qué gato! —*(CR)* (slang) Isn't he wonderful at that!

¡Qué le vamos a hacer! —It can't be helped!; There's nothing we can do about that!; That's the way the ball bounces!; That's too bad!; That's bad luck!

¡Qué macana! —*(Arg)* (slang) What a faux pas!; What a goof!

¡Qué mala pata! —What lousy luck!; What a bummer!

¡Qué metida de pata! —(slang) What a faux pas!; What a goof!

¿Qué onda? —*(Mex)* (slang) What's new?; What's going on?; What's up?

¡Qué padre! —*(Mex)* (slang) That's cool!; That's great!

¡Qué pereza! —*(CR)* What a bore!; I don't feel like it!

¡Qué poca abuela! —*(Mex)* (slang) (vulgar) What nerve!

¡Qué poca vergüenza! —What nerve!

¡Qué regada! —(slang) What a faux pas!; What a goof!

¡Qué suave! —*(Mex)* (slang) That's cool!; That's great!

¡Qué te(le) importa! —It's none of your business!

¡Qué tirada! —*(CR)* (slang) What a shame!

¡Qué va! —Certainly not!; That's not true!

¡Qué vaciado! —(slang) What a scream!

¡Qué vaina! —*(CR, Col)* (slang) What a pain!; What a bore!

quedada (n.) —*(Mex)* An old maid ▪ *¿Luisa quedada? ¡Pero si es tan guapa! Luisa an old maid? But she's so good-looking!*

quedar(se) a (para) vestir santos (v.) —To be left unmarried; to miss the last marital train; to be an old maid; to remain single (*lit.* to be left to dress figures of saints)

quedar(se) atónito(a) (v.) —To be dumbfounded

quedar bien (o mal) (v.) —1) To fit (clothing, etc.) properly (or badly) ▪ *Te queda muy bien el vestido. The dress fits you very nicely.* —2) To do a good (or bad) job ▪ *Quedaste mal en la tienda. You did a terrible job at the store.* —3) To turn out well (or badly)

quedar(se) boquiabierto(a) (v.) —To be dumbfounded ▪ *Nos quedamos boquiabiertos con su memoria. We were astounded by his memory.*

quedar(se) con las ganas (v.) —To feel like doing (something) and be unable to ▪ *Ya no hay whisky. Parece que me voy a quedar con las ganas. There's no more whiskey. I guess I'll have to do without it.*

quedar(se) corto(a) (v.) —*(Mex)* Used when a person makes an understatement ▪ *Me dijiste que Ana es bonita. Te quedaste corto. No es bonita, es bellísima. You told me Ana is pretty. Pretty is nothing. She is gorgeous!*

quedar(se) en ayunas (v.) —To be out of it; not to know what's going on (*lit.* to go without breakfast) ▪ *¿Qué dijo Guy? No entiendo muy bien el francés y me quedé en ayunas. What did Guy say? I don't understand French very well and I didn't get the gist of it.*

quedar(se) sin guita (v.) —*(Arg)* (slang) To be broke

quejumbres (n.) —Complaining; said of a person who crabs a lot, a grouch ▪ *¡No seas tan quejumbres! Don't crab so much!*

quemar(se) (v.) —(slang) To do (something) that makes a very bad impression (*lit.* to burn yourself) ▪ *Perdimos dos clientes por la forma en que los trató Pancho. Obviamente se quemó en la empresa. Two clients were lost because of the way Pancho treated them. Obviously, his name is now mud at the company.*

quemar(se) las pestañas (v.) —To burn the midnight oil (*lit.* to burn your eyelashes with the candle flame, presumably when studying late at night)

¡Quién quita! —I suppose it's not impossible!

quilombo (n.) *(Arg)* (slang) —1) A mess; a messy situation —2) Whorehouse

quinta (n.) —A country house; a couple of acres of fruit trees; a retreat, with a few trees

R

rajar(se) (v.) —1) *(Mex)* (slang) To go back on your word *(lit.* to split open) ▪ **Roberto iba a venir conmigo, pero se rajó.** *Roberto was going to come with me, but he went back on his word.* —2) *(Mex)* To give up; to surrender ▪ **Ya no aguanto más. Me rajo.** *I can't take it anymore. I give up.* —3) *(Arg)* To leave ▪ **Rajé pa' no llorar.** *I left to keep from crying.* (Lyrics of a famous tango)

rajón (rajona) (n.) —*(Mex)* (slang) A person who backs out of a deal ▪ **No creas en la palabra de Mario, es un rajón.** *Don't trust Mario. He doesn't keep his word.*

ranazo (n.) —*(Mex)* (slang) A painful fall

rascabuchear (v.) —*(Cuba)* (slang) To stare lasciviously at a girl

rascar(se) con sus propias uñas (v.) —To fend for yourself; to go it alone *(lit.* to scratch yourself with your own nails)

rascuache (adj.) —*(Mex)* (slang) Crummy; cheap; tacky

rasgar(se) (v.) —*(Col)* (slang) To kick the bucket; to die ▪ **El muchacho de repente se rasgó.** *The guy suddenly kicked the bucket.*

rata (n.) —(slang) Thief

ratón (n.) —1) *(Ven)* (slang) A hangover —2) *(Mex)* Petty thief; pickpocket *(lit.* mouse)

rebambaramba (n.) —*(Cuba)* (slang) A big to-do about something

rebotar (v.) —(slang) To bounce (used for checks only) ▪ **Me rebotaron el cheque por falta de fondos.** *The check bounced.*

recunteques (n.) —*(Peru)* Flourishes in a dance step; flourishes in playing a guitar piece ▪ **Hacía vibrar la guitarra con bellos recunteques.** *He played the guitar with beautiful flourishes.*

regar(la) (v.) —*(Mex)* (slang) To put your foot in it; to screw things up ▪ **La riega por hacer todo sin cuidado.** *He screws things up because he's so careless.*

(un) resto (n.) —*(Mex)* A whole lot ▪ **Hay un resto de dinero en ese cajón.** *There's a whole lot of money in that drawer.*

retachar (v.) —To send back

retrucar(le) a (alguien) (v.) —*(Arg)* To reply to (someone); to talk back at (someone)

rollo (n.) —A convoluted and confusing explanation (often used when giving excuses); a bunch of bull

---

ruco(a) (n.) (adj.)—*(CR, Mex)* (slang) Old (people only); an old nag
- *Tu abuelo ya está muy ruco.* *Your grandfather is very old.*

rumba (n.) —*(Col)* (slang) A party

rumbiar (v.) —*(Col)* (slang) To paint the town red

(una) runfla de (algo) (n.) —A group of undesirable people; riffraff
- *Me sentí incómoda cuando Juan llegó con su runfla de amigotes.* *I felt uncomfortable when Juan arrived with his tacky, roughneck friends.*

saber(se) al dedillo (algo) (v.) —To know (something) perfectly; to have (something) at one's fingertips ▪ *Pregúntale a Juan. El se sabe los precios al dedillo. Ask Juan. He knows the prices by heart.*

saber lo que le conviene (v.) —To know which side your bread is buttered on

saber(selas) todas (v.) —To have the answer to everything ▪ *El jefe se las sabe todas. The boss has the answer to everything.*

sacar(le) a (algo o alguien) (v.) —To get cold feet ▪ *Ya pensé bien lo del negocio que quieres poner conmigo y de plano le saco. I've thought about the business you want to go into with me, and I'm really getting cold feet.*

sacar boleto (v.) —*(Mex)* (slang) To ask for it (usually trouble) ▪ *No sigas provocando a Jorge. Estás sacando boleto. Stop picking on Jorge. You're really asking for it!*

sacar de onda a (alguien) (v.) —*(Mex)* (slang) To confuse (someone); to throw (someone) for a loop (*lit.* to get someone off the wavelength) ▪ *Me sacó de onda Gaby. ¿Por qué estará tan triste, cuando siempre es muy alegre? I wonder why Gabby is so sad… She's such a cheerful person. That surprised me a lot.*

sacar las uñas (v.) —1) To steal (something) stealthily —2) To seem mild, then become aggressive (*lit.* to unsheathe your claws)

¡Sale!; ¡Sale y vale! —(slang) I agree!; It's a deal!; I'm with you on that!; Let's do it!

salir a (alguien) (v.) —To take after (someone) ▪ *La niña salió a su madre. The little girl takes after her mother.*

salir bailando (v.) —To get the short end of the stick (*lit.* to end up dancing) ▪ *Si Paco hace las cuentas, yo voy a salir bailando. De eso puedes estar seguro. If Paco does the accounting, you can be sure I'm going to get the short end of the stick.*

salir con (alguien) (v.) —To go out with (someone); to go steady with (someone)

salir(se) con la suya (v.) —To get away with it; to get your way (*lit.* to end up having your way) ▪ *Ese Arturo es muy hábil. Pensé que lo iban a descubrir, pero se salió con la suya. Arturo is very crafty. I thought they were going to catch him, but he got away with it.*

salir del paso (v.) —To do (something) just to get out of a tight spot ▪ *No va a venir. Nada más dijo que sí para salir del paso. He is not com-*

ing. He just said yes to get out of a tight spot.

salir disparado(a) (v.) —To make a beeline…

salir hecho(a) la mocha (v.) —*(Mex)* (slang) To make a beeline…

salir hecho(a) la raya (v.) —*(Mex)* (slang) To make a beeline…

salir volando con todo y jaula (v.) —*(Ven)* (slang) To have a lot of smarts (*lit.* to fly off, cage and all) ▪ *Juan sale volando con todo y jaula. Juan is one sharp cookie.*

sangrón (sangrona) (adj.) —*(Mex)* To be boring or obnoxious (people only); a jerk ▪ *No traigas al sangrón de tu primo. Don't bring your cousin. He's such a bore.*

sangronada (n.) —*(Mex)* (slang) An obnoxious act

sapear a (alguien) (v.) —*(Col)* (slang) To make (someone) look bad; to accuse (someone)

se me hace que … —I bet … ▪ *Tomás se reportó enfermo, pero a mí se me hace que se fue a la playa. Tomas called in sick. Want to bet he went off to the beach?*

seguir(le) la corriente a (alguien) (v.) —To humor (someone); to go along with (someone)

sentir(se) apachurrado(a) (v.) —To be down in the dumps

sentir(se) de maravilla (v.) —To feel like a million dollars

sentir(se) en confianza (v.) —To let your hair down

sentir(se) la mamá de los pollitos (v.) —To feel self-important, self-satisfied (*lit.* to feel that you're the mother of the little chicks) ▪ *Lola es bastante guapa, pero se siente la mamá de los pollitos. Lola is more or less good-looking, but she thinks she's quite something.*

sentir(se) muy sabroso(a) (v.) —*(Mex)* (slang) To feel that you're superior, or very good or unbeatable at (something) when that is not always the case (*lit.* to feel that you're yummy) ▪ *Ese policía se siente muy sabroso. That policeman thinks he's very cool.*

ser abusado(a) (v.) —*(Mex)* (slang) To be sharp, alert (corruption of **aguzado**: sharp)

ser amarrete (v.) —*(Arg, Peru)* (slang) To be stingy

ser aplicado(a) (v.) —To be very studious

ser arrancado(a) (v.) —*(CR)* (slang) To do things without thinking ▪ *Pagaste antes de comprobar que se debía. Eres muy arrancado. You just paid up without stopping to find out if you really owed that much. You're* *always doing things without thinking.*

ser asomado(a) (v.) —*(Ven)* (slang) To be a busybody

ser atorado(a) (v.) —*(Ven)* (slang) To be a person who is always rushing around ineffectually ▪ *María corre sin parar por toda la ciudad, y hace muy pocas cosas. Es muy atorada.* Maria is always dashing here and there all over the city, but gets very little done. She's a busy little featherbrain.

ser balaca (v.) —*(Ecu)* (slang) To be a loudmouthed show-off

ser barbero(a) (v.) —To be the kind of person who sucks up to or brownnoses others

ser buena gente (v.) —To be a great guy (gal) ▪ *Gracias por ofrecerte a prestarme tu coche. Eres muy buena gente.* Thanks for offering to lend me your car. You're a nice guy.

ser cabeza de ratón (v.) —To be a big fish in a small pond

ser cara dura (v.) —To be the kind of person who does outrageous, rude or selfish things with no consideration and no feelings of guilt ▪ *No hagas lo que te pide Raúl. Es muy cara dura.* Don't do anything Raul asks you to. He's pushy and crass.

ser (un) cero a la izquierda (v.) —To be totally useless (people only) (*lit.* to be a zero on the left of a figure) ▪ *Nadie le hace caso. Es cero a la izquierda.* Nobody pays him the slightest attention. He's a nitwit.

ser como sacarle jugo a un riel (v.) —*(CR)* To be stingy; to be a real tightwad (*lit.* it's like getting juice out of a rail) ▪ *Es muy tacaño. Sacarle dinero es como sacarle jugo a un riel.* He is extremely stingy. Getting money out of him is almost impossible.

ser conchudo(a) (v.) —(slang) To have a lot of nerve

ser corriente (v.) —To be very ordinary or of poor quality (things); to be ill-bred or to have bad manners (people) ▪ *Se comporta mal. Es muy corriente.* He behaves badly. He's very crass (ill-bred).

ser chinche (v.) —To be the kind of person who makes others waste time

ser chiva (v.) —1) *(CR)* (slang) To be a neat person ▪ *Gloria es muy chiva.* Gloria is very neat. —2) *(Mex)* To be the type of person who goes back on his/her word

ser de buen comer (v.) —To enjoy eating; to have a good appetite

ser de buena madera (v.) —To be made of good material (physically; used for people)

ser de buena pasta (v.) —To be made of good material (physically;

---

used for people)

ser de una pieza (v.) —To have unbreakable integrity ■ *No se deja soborna. Es de una pieza. He can't be bribed. His integrity is rock solid.*

ser del año de la canica (v.) —(slang) To be as old as the hills (*lit.* to date back to the year in which marbles were invented) ■ *Ya quiero deshacerme de este traje. Es del año de la canica. I want to get rid of this suit. It's as old as the hills.*

ser del año del caldo (v.) —(slang) To be as old as the hills (*lit.* to date back to the year in which broth was invented)

ser del montón (v.) —To be ordinary, common, mediocre (*lit.* to be of the heap)

ser encajoso(a) (v.) —(slang) To take unfair advantage of (someone) ■ *En esta tienda son muy encajosos. ¡Querían 20 pesos por un refresco! They always overcharge me at this store. They wanted 20 pesos for a soft drink!*

ser espléndido(a) (v.) —To be extremely generous

ser flojo(a) (v.) —To be lazy (*lit.* to be limp)

ser fodongo(a) (v.) —(slang) To be lazy (and sometimes dirty or messy as well)

ser fresa (v.) —(slang) To be a goody two-shoes

ser gagá (v.) —*(Peru)* (slang) To be a goody-goody ■ *Jorge es un chico de lo más gagá. Jorge is a total square.*

ser (algo) hecho y derecho (v.) —To be every inch a (something) ■ *Luisito ya es un hombre hecho y derecho. Luisito is every inch a man.*

ser la gota que derramó el vaso (v.) —To be the last straw (*lit.* to be the drop that overflowed the glass) ■ *Le aguanté todo a mi socio, pero decirme tramposo fue la gota que derramó el vaso. I put up with a lot from my partner, but calling me a cheat is the last straw!*

ser la manzana de la discordia (v.) —To be a bone of contention

ser la niña de los ojos de (alguien) (v.) —To be the apple of (someone's) eye ■ *Jimena es preciosa y simpática. Con razón es la niña de los ojos de su papá. Jimena is adorable and charming. No wonder she's the apple of her daddy's eye.*

ser la piel de Judas (v.) —To be a holy terror (*lit.* to be the skin of Judas)

ser lengua de gato (v.) —*(CR)* (slang) To be (someone) who can't tolerate hot food (temp.; does not refer to spicy food, such as chilies)

ser líder charro (v.) —*(Mex)* To be a union leader who sells out to company management ▪ *Muchos sindicatos tienen líderes charros. Many unions have union bosses who are hand in glove with company management.*

ser liso(a) (v.) —*(Ven)* (slang) To be the type of person who is too chummy ▪ *¡Oye, tu primo es un liso! Your cousin is really a little too chummy!*

ser lisuriento(a) (v.) —*(Peru)* (slang) To be a foulmouthed person

ser macanero(a) (v.) —*(Arg)* (slang) To be a liar

ser malora (v.) —*(Mex)* (slang) To be (someone) who likes to bother or pick on people

ser más agarrado que un moño en un ventolero (v.) —*(CR)* (slang) To be stingy; to be a real tightwad *(lit.* to hold on as tightly as a bow in a windstorm)

ser más largo que las orejas de un burro (v.) —*(CR)* To be extremely long; endless (used for physical things and events) *(lit.* to be longer than a donkey's ears)

ser más largo que un domingo sin plata (v.) —*(CR)* To be extremely long; endless *(lit.* to be longer than a Sunday with no money)

ser metiche (v.) —(slang) To be a busybody

ser mosca (mosquita) muerta (v.) —To be a dull and inconspicuous person on the surface *(lit.* to be a dead fly)

ser mucha hembra (v.) —(slang) To be a complete woman; to be a #10 with brains (good-looking, bright, assertive, self-reliant, etc.)

ser mucho camisón pa' Petra (v.) —*(Ven)* To be out of your depth; to be unable to handle a job or situation ▪ *Ese puesto en el banco es mucho camisón pa' Petra. That job at the bank is more than he can handle.*

ser (muy) mula (v.) —*(Mex)* To be mean *(lit.* to be a mule)

ser muy acá (v.) —*(Mex)* (slang) To be very snooty and standoffish

ser muy fijado(a) (v.) —To notice everything; to be very critical

ser muy mujer (v.) —(slang) To be an excellent housekeeper

ser natural de (lugar) (v.) —To be a native of a place ▪ *Era natural de Asturias. He was a native of Asturias.*

ser pepón (v.) —*(Peru)* To be a fine figure of a man

ser petiso(a) (v.) —*(Arg)* (slang) To be chubby

ser picudo(a) (v.) —*(Mex)* (slang) To be a whiz at something

ser pipa (v.) —1) *(CR)* To be a good student; to be studious *(lit.* to be an unpeeled coconut) ▪ *Jaime es muy pipa. Jaime is a wonderful student.* —2) *(Mex)* (slang) To be a drunkard

ser (de) pipí cogido (v.) —*(CR)* (slang) To be extremely good friends ▪ *Juan y Carlos son de pipí cogido. Juan and Carlos are best buddies.*

ser (un(a)) pisapasito (v.) —*(Ven)* (slang) To be a dull and inconspicuous person on the surface

ser popis (v.) —*(Mex)* (slang) To be a member of high society

ser quisquilloso(a) (v.) —To be very fastidious; to be picky

ser sangre de chinche (adj.) —*(Ven)* (slang) To be boring or obnoxious (people only); to be a jerk

ser torpe de manos (v.) —To be all thumbs

ser traga años (v.) —To look a lot younger than you really are

ser un avión (v.) —*(Col)* (slang) To be the type of person who uses others unscrupulously

ser un bucha (v.) —*(Cuba)* (slang) To be a despicable person

ser un cafisio (v.) —*(Arg)* (slang) To be a gigolo

ser un compadrito (v.) —*(Arg)* (slang) To be a stud; to be a show-off

ser un cuero (v.) —*(Mex)* (slang) To be handsome or good-looking (both sexes) (*lit.* to be a piece of hide)

ser un don nadie (v.) —To be a nobody

ser un estuche de monerías (v.) —To be accomplished in many different skills (*lit.* to be a chest full of cute abilities)

ser un(a) fregado(a) (v.) —*(Gua)* (slang) To be bad-tempered

ser un jamón (v.) —*(Cuba)* (slang) To be extremely easy ▪ *El examen fue un jamón. The test was a breeze.*

ser un mango (v.) —(slang) To be handsome or good-looking (both sexes) (*lit.* to be a ripe, luscious, juicy fruit)

ser un palucha (v.) —*(Cuba)* (slang) To be a loudmouthed show-off

ser un pan de Dios (v.) —To be a truly good person (*lit.* to be a piece of God's bread)

ser un(a) pelado(a) (v.) —*(Mex)* (slang) To be (someone) who uses bad language

ser un plomo (v.) —1) *(Mex)* (slang) To be dull, uninteresting and unpleasant (people only); to be a jerk —2) *(Arg)* To be a helper (*lit.* to be a piece of lead)

ser un pozo de sabiduría (v.) —To be a bottomless pit of wisdom

ser un(a) rompebolas (v.) —*(Arg, Uru)* (slang, vulgar) To be a nuisance

ser un(a) tal por cual (v.) —To be a bastard, a mean person ▪ *Javier es un tal por cual. Javier is a real bastard.*

ser un tipo de avería (v.) —*(Arg)* (slang) To be (someone) not to be trusted

ser una ficha (v.) —(slang) (people only) To be crooked (to varying degrees)

ser una ladilla (v.) —*(Mex)* (vulgar) To be a nuisance

ser una lata (v.) —To be a pain or bother

ser una monserga (v.) —To be very annoying; to be a pain

ser una nata (v.) —(slang) To be totally inept, useless (*lit.* to be like the skin that forms on boiled milk)

ser una papaya (v.) —*(Chi)* (slang) To be extremely easy ▪ *El examen fue una papaya. The test was a breeze.*

ser una perdida (v.) —To be a loose woman (*lit.* to be a lost woman) ▪ *Su amiga es una perdida. Your friend is a loose woman.*

ser una plasta (v.) —To be a total nitwit

ser una tempestad en un vaso de agua (v.) —To be a tempest in a teapot

serruchar(le) el piso a (alguien) (v.) —*(CR)* (slang) To screw (someone); to harm (someone); to outwit (someone) (*lit.* to saw a hole in the floor around someone) ▪ *Juan le está serruchando el piso a Miguel. Juan is trying to screw Miguel.*

serruchar(le) la gamba a (alguien) (v.) —*(Arg)* (slang) To play a dirty trick on (someone)

si se va a hacer negro, que sea trompudo —*(CR)* (slang) If you're going to go to the trouble, go all out!

siempre no —When (something) is not going to be done after all ▪ *¿Te acuerdas de la fiesta que estábamos planeando? Pues dice mi mamá que siempre no. Remember the party we were planning? Well, my mother says it's off.*

siempre sí —When (something) is going to be done after all ▪ *Ayer me cancelaron el pedido. Ahora resulta que siempre sí lo quieren. Yesterday, they canceled the order. Now it turns out they want it after all.*

sin decir agua va (adv.) —*(Mex)* Without warning ▪ *¡Me cambió de equipo sin decir agua va! He switched me to another team with no warning at all!*

sin pena ni gloria (adv.) —So-so; not outstanding; run of the mill

- *Fue un juego sin pena ni gloria.* It was not an outstanding game.

sin rodeos (adv.) —Straight from the hip; without beating around the bush

sin ton ni son (adv.) —Without rhyme or reason; making no sense

sobre manera (adv.) —Very much ■ *Le agradezco sobre manera. I appreciate this very much.*

soltar(se) las trenzas (v.) —*(Chi)* Not to care about something

sonar(se) (v.) —To blow your nose ■ *No te suenes en la mesa. Don't blow your nose at the table.*

sonar(se) a (alguien) (v.) —1) *(Mex)* (slang) To beat (someone) up ■ *Carlos se sonó a Jaime. Carlos beat up Jaime.* —2) To spank (someone) ■ *Le voy a tener que sonar a ese niño malcriado. I'm going to have to spank that brat.*

sudar(le) el copete (v.) —(slang) To have a hard time; to sweat blood; to get in a sweat (*lit.* to get sweat on your brow)

sudar la gota gorda (v.) —To have a hard time; to sweat blood; to get in a sweat (*lit.* to sweat fat drops of perspiration) ■ *Llevo todo el día en esto y todavía faltan diez canastas. Estoy sudando la gota gorda. I've been at this all day and there are still six baskets to go. I'm having a really hard time here.*

sudar tinta (v.) —To have a hard time; to sweat blood; to get in a sweat (*lit.* to sweat ink)

sulfurar(se) (v.) —*(Mex)* To get all upset ■ *Está bien, mañana te pago lo que te debo. ¡No te sulfures! OK, I'll pay you what I owe you tomorrow. Don't get all upset!*

taco (n.) —*(Chi)* (slang) A mess; a messy situation

tal cual (adv.) —As is; just as it is; exactly the same ▪ *Déjame esos papeles tal cual.* *Leave those papers there just as they are.*

tambache (n.) —*(Mex)* (slang) Bundle of clothes or other stuff

tan es así, que … —So much so that … ▪ *Carla y Teo de veras se odian. Tan es así, que Carla no quiso ir a la boda de Fabián porque supo que Teo iba.* *Carla and Teo really despise each other. So much so that Carla refused to go to Fabian's wedding because she knew Teo would be there.*

tapar(le) el ojo al macho (v.) —To make a vain attempt to hide something ▪ *Es inútil tratar de ocultar el faltante. No podemos taparle el ojo al macho.* *It's no use trying to cover up the missing money. We can't keep it from becoming known.*

tender(le) una trampa a (alguien) (v.) —To set a trap for (someone)

tener (traer) botado de (la) risa a (alguien) (v.) —To have (someone) in stitches (*lit.* to make someone bounce with laughter) ▪ *Raúl tiene botadas de la risa a todas las niñas del salón.* *Raul has all the girls in the classroom in stitches.*

tener buena cara (v.) —To look good or appealing (both persons and things) (*lit.* to have a good face) ▪ *Mira estas enchiladas. Tienen muy buena cara.* *Look at these enchiladas. They look really good.*

tener cara dura (v.) —To have a lot of nerve ▪ *¡Vaya que tiene cara dura! ¡Agarró el último taco, y Elsa no había comido nada!* *Boy, he sure has some nerve! He grabbed the last taco, and Elsa hadn't eaten anything!*

tener carita de pena (v.) —*(Ecu)* To look worried

tener cola que le pisen (v.) —To have skeletons in the closet ▪ *No pudo protestar por los abusos de su compañero, porque tiene cola que le pisen.* *He just couldn't report what his cellmate was doing, because he had his own dark secrets.*

tener colmillo (v.) —*(Mex)* (slang) To be very savvy and smart ▪ *No es fácil tomarle el pelo. Tiene mucho colmillo.* *It's not easy to fool him. He's a smart cookie.*

tener comiendo de la mano a (alguien) (v.) —To wrap (someone) around your little finger (*lit.* to have someone eating out of your hand) ▪ *Nunca había visto así a Miguel. Lo tienes comiendo de la mano.* *I've never seen Miguel like that. You've got him eating out of your hand.*

tener (mucha) concha (v.) —(slang) To have a lot of nerve ▪ *Pepe se* *llevó el coche sin permiso. ¡Tiene mucha concha!* Pepe took the car without permission. He has a lot of nerve!

tener cuña (v.) —*(Arg, Chi)* (slang) To have pull (*lit.* to have a wedge) ▪ *Luis tiene cuña en el Ministerio.* Luis has pull at the Ministry.

tener (su) chiste (v.) —(slang) To be no simple matter; to be complicated, tricky, or hard to do ▪ *Bordar con esa perfección tiene su chiste.* Embroidering like that is no simple matter.

tener chiva (v.) —*(Ven)* (slang) To be lucky

tener chorro (chorrillo) (v.) —To have the runs

tener don de gentes (v.) —To have a pleasant personality; to be the kind of person that everyone likes to deal with or talk to ▪ *En este trabajo hay que tener don de gentes para lograr el éxito.* To succeed in this job, you must have the knack of dealing with people.

tener el cuarto lleno de agua (v.) —*(Ven)* To be in hot water; to be up to here; to be at the breaking point

tener el cuerpo molido (v.) —To be worn out; to be exhausted

tener el presentimiento de (algo) (v.) —To feel (something) in your bones ▪ *Tengo el presentimiento de que no va a venir.* I have a feeling that he is not coming.

tener en cuenta (algo) (v.) —To keep (something) in mind

tener en el bolsillo a (alguien) (v.) —To wrap (someone) around your little finger (*lit.* to have someone in your pocket)

tener ganas de (algo); tener ganas de hacer (algo) (v.) —To be appealing; to feel like doing something

tener lengua viperina (v.) —To speak ill of other people (*lit.* to have the tongue of a snake)

tener mala leche (v.) —To have a mean streak

tener presente a (alguien o algo) (v.) —To have (someone or something) on your mind

tener que bajar el moño (v.) —*(Chi)* (slang) To eat crow ▪ *No pude decir nada para defenderme, así que tuve que bajar el moño.* I could say nothing to defend myself, so I had to eat crow.

tener sangre de atole (v.) —*(Mex)* To have no gumption (*lit.* to have blood made of **atole** (corn gruel))

tener sencillo (v.) —*(Gua)* To have small change (coins)

tener sentido (v.) —To make sense

tener su lado bueno (v.) —To have a silver lining; to have a good side ▪ *Hay fracasos que tienen su lado bueno. There are failures that have a silver lining (a good side).*

tener sus bemoles (v.) —To have its cons; to have its problems; to be complex and difficult (*lit.* to have flat notes (in music)) ▪ *Manejar bien una computadora, tiene sus bemoles. Proper handling of a computer is rather complex and difficult.*

tener (haber) tela de dónde cortar (v.) —To have enough of (something) to work with; to have all kinds of possibilities (*lit.* to have material to cut from) ▪ *Debes reducir tu discurso, que es bueno pero muy largo. Hay tela de dónde cortar. Your speech should be shortened. It's too long, but there is a lot of good material in it.*

tener un barniz de (algo) (v.) —To have a smattering of knowledge about something

tener un cajón de sastre (v.) —*(Chi)* (slang) To have your belongings in a mess, not neat and tidy

tener metejón (v.) —*(Arg)* (slang) To be passionately in love; to be hooked on something

tener un trabajo de locos (v.) —To be loaded with work

tener una mina (v.) —*(Arg)* (slang) To have a sweetheart

tener una movida (v.) —*(Mex)* (slang) To have a date which is either for sex pure and simple, or will end up in bed (not a romantic date) (*lit.* to have a move)

tener vara alta (v.) —To have pull (*lit.* to have a high stick)

tipejo(a) (n.) —A third-rate, low-down bum; a louse ▪ *Juan Antonio es un tipejo. Juan Antonio is nothing but a louse.*

tirar (de) a loco (lucas) (v.) —To ignore ▪ *Lolita no me hace caso. Me tira de a loco. Lolita pays no attention to me. She just ignores me.*

tirar la casa por la ventana (v.) —To go all out

tirar(se) la parada (v.) —*(Ven)* (slang) To take a risk ▪ *Ustedes váyanse. Yo me tiro la parada. You go. I'll assume the risk.*

tirar(se) la pera (v.) —*(Chi)* (slang) To lounge around doing nothing

tirar(le) plancha a (alguien) (v.) —To leave (someone) waiting

(un) titipuchal (n.) —*(Mex)* (slang) A whole lot; a bunch

tocar (v.) —*(Cuba)* (slang) To bribe

todo el santo día (adv.) —All the livelong day; the whole day long

---

¡Todo fuera como eso! —*(Mex)* If that were the worst of my problems!; that's a really insignificant problem! ▪ *¿Te faltan 10 pesos? ¡Todo fuera como eso! Yo te los doy. You're short ten pesos? If that were the worst of our problems!! Here, I'll give them to you.*

tomar a pecho (algo) (v.) —To take (something) seriously; to be hurt or offended by something; to take (something) to heart (*lit.* to take something to your breast) ▪ *Carlos no sabe lo que dice. No lo tomes tan a pecho. Carlos doesn't know what he's talking about. Don't take it so seriously.*

tomar(le) el pelo a (alguien) (v.) —To pull (someone's) leg (*lit.* to take someone's hair) ▪ *No lo tomes en serio. Te están tomando el pelo. Don't take it so seriously. They're pulling your leg.*

tomar(se) el trabajo de (algo) (v.) —To take or to go to the trouble; to bother ▪ *Se tomó el trabajo de lavar los trastes y limpiarme la cocina. He went to the trouble of washing the dishes and cleaning up the kitchen for me.*

tomar en cuenta a (alguien o algo) (v.) —To keep (someone or something) in mind while making a decision; to consider (someone's) opinion or presence

tomar(se) la molestia (v.) —To take or to go to the trouble; to bother ▪ *Se tomó la molestia de llevarme al aeropuerto. He went to the trouble of taking me to the airport.*

torpedo (n.) —*(Chi)* A crib sheet; secret notes to copy from in a test

trabar(se) de coraje (v.) —To see red

trácala (n.) —*(Mex)* (slang) A scam ▪ *Cuídate de su hermano, es muy trácala. Look out for yourself when his brother is around. He's really crooked.*

tracalero (adj.) —*(Mex)* (slang) A crooked person ▪ *Tu primo es un tracalero. Your cousin is a crook.*

traer cortito(a) a (alguien) (v.) —To have (someone) on a short leash ▪ *No puedo llegar ni cinco minutos tarde. Me traen cortito. I can't even be five minutes late! They've got me on a short leash!*

traer(le) ganas a (alguien) (v.) —1) To want to beat up or kill someone ▪ *Ese tipo me trae ganas porque bailé con su novia. That guy has it in for me because I danced with his girlfriend.* —2) To want to get (someone) into bed ▪ *Es muy obvio que Alberto le trae ganas a Rosalía. It's very obvious that Alberto has the hots for Rosalía.*

traer la lengua de corbata (v.) —To be worn out; to be exhausted (*lit.* to have your tongue hanging out like a man's tie)

traer marcando el paso a (alguien) (v.) —To have (someone) on a

short leash ▪ *Ese niño es tan educadito, porque siempre lo traen mar-*
cando el paso. *That kid is so well mannered because his parents are very strict*
with him.

traer una mamúa (v.) —*(Arg)* (slang) To be drunk ▪ *Norberto trae una*
mamúa buena. *Norberto is plastered.*

¡Trágame tierra! —I'm so embarrassed, I could die! (*lit.* Swallow me,
Earth!)

tragar camote (v.) —1) *(Mex)* (slang) To be unable to do something or
handle a situation; to be petrified (*lit.* to swallow yam) ▪ *No te quedes*
allí tragando camote, ¡ayúdame! Don't just stand there looking stupid. Come
and help me! —2) To eat crow ▪ *No pude decir nada para defenderme, así*
que tuve que tragar camote. I could say nothing to defend myself, so I had to
eat crow.

tragar(se) el anzuelo (v.) —To swallow (something) hook, line and
sinker

tragar(se) la tierra a (alguien o algo) (v.) —To disappear (*lit.* to be
swallowed up by the earth) ▪ *No volví a verlo. Se lo tragó la tierra. I*
never saw him again. He simply vanished.

trajinar (v.) —1) *(Cuba)* (slang) To play practical jokes —2) *(Mex)* To
work

tramafax (n.) —*(ES)* (slang) A deceitful act

trancar (v.) —*(CR)* To lock (*lit.* to bolt)

tranque (n.) —*(Cuba)* (slang) A mess; a messy situation

¡Trato hecho! —It's a deal!

treques (n.) —*(Ecu, PR, DR, Pan)* (slang) Things; thingamajigs; stuff; junk

trincar a (alguien) (v.) —*(Ecu)* (slang) To catch (someone) red-handed

triques (n.) —*(Mex)* (slang) Things; thingamajigs; stuff; junk

tronar (algo) (v.) —(slang) To blow; to ruin; to screw up (something)
▪ *Jorge tronó el coche por no ponerle aceite. Jorge ruined (screwed up) the*
car 'cause he never put any oil in it.

tronar(se) (dinero) (v.) —(slang) To blow (money) ▪ *Jorge se tronó toda*
su quincena apostando. Jorge blew his whole salary payment at the gambling
table.

tronar a (con) (alguien) (v.) —(slang) To break up with (someone)
▪ *Lourdes tronó con Jaime. Lourdes gave Jaime the heave-ho.*

tronco (n.) —*(Ven)* (slang) A person with a really attractive body; a hunk
▪ *¡Mira qué tronco de mujer! Look at that gorgeous broad!*

U

(el) último grito (de la moda) (n.) —The latest rage in fashion

untar(le) la mano a (alguien) (v.) —To bribe; to grease (someone's) palm

V

vaciado(a) (adj.) —(slang) Amusing; entertaining; funny ▪ *El novio de Sandra es vaciado. Sandra's boyfriend is very amusing.*

vacilar (v.) —1) To wander or be confused —2) (slang) To pull (someone's) leg; to joke around ▪ *El maestro siempre nos está vacilando. The teacher is always pulling our leg.*

vacilón (n.) —(slang) A fun time ▪ *Ando de vacilón con mis cuates. I'm having a blast with my pals.*

vaina (n.) —*(Col)* (slang) A complicated or irritating situation

valer(le) gorro a (alguien) (v.) —*(Mex)* (slang) Not to care; not to give a damn ▪ *¿Crees que me importa si te vas? ¡Me vale gorro! You think I care if you leave? I couldn't care less!*

valer la pena (v.) —To be worthwhile (*lit.* to be worth the pain) ▪ *Es un libro largo y difícil, pero de veras vale la pena. It's a long, difficult book, but it's really worth it.*

valer(le) riata a (alguien) (v.) —*(ES)* (slang) Not to care; not to give a damn ▪ *¿Te vas? Me vale riata. You're leaving. I don't care!*

valer(le) sombrilla a (alguien) (v.) —*(Mex)* (slang) Not to care; not to give a damn

¡Válgame Dios! —Dear me!; Dear God!; God help us!; Oh my God!; Well, I'll be…!

vamos bien —So far, so good

varo(s) (n.) —*(Mex)* Bucks ($)

¡Vaya! —Well!; Well, well!; So!; It's about time!

venir(le) bien (v.) —1) To suit (someone); to be convenient or helpful ▪ *Ese horario me viene muy bien. That schedule is very convenient.* —2) To fit; to be becoming ▪ *El vestido azul te viene muy bien. The blue dress really becomes you.*

venir disparado(a) (v.) —(slang) To come over in a great hurry (*lit.* to come over like a shot)

venir hecho(a) la mocha (v.) —*(Mex)* (slang) To come over like a streak ▪ *Llegó a tiempo porque vino hecho la mocha.* *He arrived on time, because he came over like a streak.*

venir(le) mal (v.) —To be inconvenient ▪ *La hora de esa cita me viene muy mal.* *The time of that appointment is not at all convenient for me.*

venir mandado(a) (v.) —*(Cuba, Chi)* (slang) To go lickety-split; to fly

venir muy currutaco (v.) —*(Arg)* (slang) To be all dressed up

venir volando (volado(a)) (v.) —(slang) To come like a shot

ver(se) a la legua (v.) —To be very obvious (*lit.* to be visible from a mile away) ▪ *Se ve a la legua su interés por el dinero.* *His interest in the money is as clear as day.*

ver(le) la cara (de tonto(a)) a (alguien) (v.) —To fool (someone) (*lit.* to realize from someone's face that he/she is easy to fool) ▪ *No me digan que afinaron este coche. ¿Creen que me van a ver cara de tonto?* *You say you tuned up this car? You think you can fool me?*

ver(le) la oreja blanca a (alguien) (v.) —*(Ven)* (slang) To fool (someone) (*lit.* to see someone's white ear)

ver(le) las canillas a (alguien) (v.) —*(Chi)* To fool (someone) (*lit.* to see someone's shins) ▪ *¿Me quieres ver las canillas?* *Are you trying to put one over on me?*

ver los toros desde la barrera (v.) —To avoid getting involved; to be an onlooker when there is trouble (*lit.* to watch the bullfight from the safety of the spectator's stalls)

ver moros con tranchetes (v.) —To imagine danger or trouble where there is none (*lit.* to see Moors with battle axes) ▪ *No es cierto que el gerente quiera despedirte. Estás viendo moros con tranchetes.* *It's not true that the manager wants to fire you. You're imagining things!*

verraco (n.) —*(Col)* (slang) A daring person

verraquería (n.) —*(Col)* (slang) (something) super

vivales (n.) —A crooked operator

vivir al día (v.) —To live from day to day; to live from hand to mouth

vivir en un conventillo (v.) —*(Arg)* To live in a low-income apartment or house, such as a tenement

volada (n.) —A feat

---

volar(se) (algo) (v.) —*(Mex)* (slang) To steal, filch or pinch (something) (*lit.* to make something fly)

volar lente (volar vidrio) (v.) —*(Gua)* (slang) To spy

Y

¡Ya! —*(Peru)* Yes, I have understood what you said; Got it!

¡Ya caigo! —*(Mex)* Oh, now I get it! (when it has taken (someone) a very long time to catch on)

¡Ya estuvo bueno! —That's enough!

¡Ya estuvo suave! —*(Mex)* (slang) That's enough! Cut it out! You've gone too far! ▪ *Van seis veces que te presto dinero. ¡Ya estuvo suave! I've lent you money six times now. That's enough!*

¡Ya lo creo! —I should say so!; Of course!; Certainly!; Absolutely!; Naturally!

¡Ya llovió! —A long time ago; It's been ages...! ▪ *Ya llovió desde la última vez que nos vimos. It's been ages since we last saw each other.*

¡Ya vas! —*(Mex)* It's a deal!; OK! (I like your suggestion); Great idea!

yegua (n.) —*(Arg)* (slang) A good-looking woman ▪ *Jorge trae una yegua de muerte. Jorge is with a terrific-looking chick!*

Z

zarandajas (n.) —*(Mex)* Doodads; baubles

zarandajo(a) (n.) —*(Ven)* (slang) A lazy bum

Phrases and Expressions in English

A

Absolutely! —¡**Por supuesto!**

act of God —**Desastre natural; caso de fuerza mayor**

to add fuel to the fire —**Echar leña al fuego** ▪ *To ask for the ring back would just add fuel to the fire.* **Pedirle que te devuelva el anillo sería echar leña al fuego.**

to add insult to injury —**Como (Por) si fuera poco** ▪ *And to add insult to injury, she started flirting with my boyfriend.* **Y como si fuera poco, se puso a coquetear con mi novio.**

to air your dirty laundry in public —**Sacar los trapos (trapitos) al sol** ▪ *You know how I hate airing our dirty laundry in public.* **Ya sabes cómo odio sacar nuestros trapitos al sol.**

all of a sudden —**De repente; de pronto; de buenas a primeras** ▪ *All of a sudden, I felt ill.* **Me sentí mal de repente (de pronto; de buenas a primeras).**

an all-time high —**Sin precedentes; más alto que nunca** ▪ *Crime is at an all-time high.* **El crimen está en un nivel sin precedentes (más alto que nunca).**

Are you kidding? —¿**Está(s) bromeando?; ¿En serio?**

as a matter of fact —**De hecho; es más** ▪ *Yes, I know Dave. As a matter of fact, we work together.* **Sí, conozco a Dave. Es más, trabajamos juntos.**

as the crow flies —**En línea recta** (*lit.* in a straight line)

as usual —1) **Como de costumbre** ▪ *I'll have the soup du jour, as usual.* **Tomaré la sopa del día, como de costumbre.** —2) (sarcastic) **Para variar** (for a change) ▪ *Ana is late again, as usual.* **Ana llega otra vez tarde, para variar.**

to ask for it —**Buscar(se) un problema; ganár(sela) a pulso** ▪ *You're asking for it!* ¡**Te estás buscando un problema!** (¡**Te la estás ganando a pulso!**)

at last —**Por fin**

at least —**Por lo menos; cuando menos** ▪ *At least return my money.* **Por lo menos, devuélveme mi dinero.**

at once —**Inmediatamente; de inmediato; luego, luego**

at the drop of a hat —**En cualquier momento**

to badmouth (someone) —**Criticar a (alguien); echar(le) tierra a (alguien); echar pestes de (alguien)**

to barf —**Vomitar; volver el estómago;** *(Mex)* (slang) **guacarear(se);** *(Mex)* (slang) **cantar Oaxaca**

to bawl (someone) out —**Regañar severamente a (alguien); gritar(le) a (alguien)**

to be a big fish in a small pond —**Ser cabeza de ratón**

to be a bone of contention —**Ser la manzana de la discordia**

to be a busybody —**Ser metiche**

to be a far cry from —**Estar lejos de** ▪ *This house is a far cry from what I wanted.* **Esta casa está lejos de ser lo que yo quería.**

to be a feather in your cap —**Anotar(se) (un tanto); lograr un triunfo** ▪ *Laura won the prize. That's another feather in her cap.* **Laura ganó el premio. Se anotó un punto (logró un triunfo).**

to be a great guy (gal) —**Ser buena gente**

to be a show-off —**Ser presumido(a)**

to be a tempest in a teapot —**Ser una tempestad en un vaso de agua** ▪ *This silly fight is just a tempest in a teapot.* **Este pleito tonto no es más que una tempestad en un vaso de agua.**

to be able to cope with —**Poder con el paquete; poder con; poder manejar** ▪ *Don't leave all those kids here. I can't cope with them.* **No dejes aquí a todos esos niños. No puedo con ellos (con el paquete).**

to be able to do (something) blindfolded —**Poder hacer algo con los ojos cerrados** ▪ *Walter can beat you at chess blindfolded.* **Walter te gana al ajedrez con los ojos cerrados.**

to be able to make it —**Poder estar presente** ▪ *Let me know if you can make it.* **Avísame si puedes estar presente.**

to be able to tell that ... —**Se nota que ...** ▪ *You can tell she's had a facelift.* **Se le nota que se restiró la cara.**

to be about to do (something) —**Estar a punto de ...** ▪ *We were about to leave.* **Estábamos a punto de irnos.**

to be alive and kicking —**Estar vivito(a) y coleando** (*lit.* to be alive and wagging your tail)

to be all beat-up (cars) —*(Mex)* **Estar como (Parecer) muégano** (*lit.* to be like a **muégano**, a Mexican confection which is full of lumps) to be all for it —**Estar completamente a favor** ▪ *Good idea. I'm all for it. Buena idea. Estoy completamente a favor.*

to be all mixed up —**Estar completamente confundido(a) (perdido(a))**

to be all thumbs —**Ser de manos torpes; ser torpe de manos**

to be an S.O.B. —(slang) **Ser un(a) tal por cual** ▪ *I won't deal with Jaime again. He's an S.O.B. Ya no vuelvo a tratar con Jaime. Es un tal por cual.*

to be as bald as a billiard ball —**Ser calvo(a) como bola de billar**

to be as black as night —**Ser (estar) como boca de lobo; ser (estar) muy obscuro** (used only for rooms or other spaces)

to be at (someone's) beck and call —**Estar a la disposición de (alguien)**

to be at the end of your rope —**Estar desesperado(a); estar al borde de la desesperación**

to be at wit's end —**Estar al borde de la locura; estar desesperado(a)**

to be batty —**Estar demente; estar loco(a)**

to be beat —**Estar exhausto(a), muerto(a), agotado(a), rendido(a)**

to be behind —**Estar atrasado(a)** ▪ *We're behind with the payments. Estamos atrasados con los pagos.*

to be bent on (something) —**Estar empeñado(a) en (algo)** ▪ *He's bent on going to Harvard. Está empeñado en estudiar en Harvard.*

to be between a rock and a hard place —**Estar entre la espada y la pared** (*lit.* to be between the sword and the wall)

to be between the devil and the deep blue sea —**Estar entre la espada y la pared**

to be black and blue —**Estar todo amoratado(a); estar lleno de moretones**

to be black as the ace of spades —**Ser negro azabache**

to be blind as a bat —**Estar más ciego(a) que un topo** (*lit.* to be blind as a mole)

to be blue —**Estar deprimido(a)**

to be bonkers —**Estar demente; estar loco(a)**

to be bound to (+ verb) —**Ser inevitable; seguro que ...** ▪ *He's bound to lose that money. Es inevitable. Va a perder el dinero. (Seguro que va a perder el dinero.) It's bound to rain! ¡Seguro que va a llover!*

---

to be completely at sea —**Estar completamente confundido(a) (perdido(a)); ser hombre al agua;** *(Col)* **estar embejucado**

to be conceited —**Creer(se) la gran cosa; creer(se) la divina garza; dar(se) paquete** ▪ *Nobody can stand her because she's so conceited.* ***Nadie la aguanta porque se cree la gran cosa.***

to be cool —**Estar fabuloso(a);** *(Mex)* (slang) **estar padre**

to be dead to the world (asleep) —**Estar profundamente dormido(a)**

to be determined —**Estar decidido(a)** ▪ *He's determined to succeed.* ***Está decidido a triunfar.*** *He's a very determined man.* ***Es un hombre muy decidido.***

to be down in the dumps —**Estar deprimido(a)**

to be dressed to kill —**Estar con sus mejores galas; estar emperifollado(a);** *(Arg)* **estar muy currutaco(a)**

to be dressed to the nines —**Estar con sus mejores galas; estar emperifollado(a);** *(Arg)* **estar muy currutaco(a)**

to be dressed to the teeth —**Estar con sus mejores galas; estar emperifollado(a);** *(Arg)* **estar muy currutaco(a)**

to be dumbfounded —**Quedar(se) atónito(a); perder el habla; quedar(se) con la boca abierta** ▪ *Beatriz was dumbfounded.* ***Beatriz perdió el habla (se quedó atónita; boquiabierta).***

to be even —**Estar a mano**

to be falling on your face —**Estar(se) cayendo de cansancio** (fatigue)**; estar(se) cayendo de borracho(a)** (drunk) ▪ *That guy is falling on his face.* ***Ese tipo se está cayendo de cansancio (de borracho).***

to be famished —**Estar muerto(a) de hambre; estar muriéndo(se) de hambre**

to be far from —**Estar lejos de**

to be fed up —**Estar harto(a); estar hasta la coronilla;** *(Arg)* **estar podrido(a)** ▪ *I'm really fed up with this third-rate cell phone!* ***¡Estoy harto de este celular de tercera!***

to be hand in glove —**Ser uña y carne** (lit. to be nail and finger) ▪ *You know those two are hand in glove.* ***Tú sabes que esos dos son uña y carne.***

to be head over heels in love with (someone) —**Estar locamente (perdidamente) enamorado(a) de (alguien)** ▪ *Fred is head over heels in love with my sister.* ***Fred está locamente enamorado de mi hermana.***

to be hooked on —**Estar enamorado(a) de; estar fascinado(a) con** (when referring to alcohol, cigarettes, drugs, etc., use **ser adicto(a) a)**

- *I'm really hooked on sailing.* **Estoy fascinado con el veleo.**

to be in —**Estar de moda** ▪ *Long skirts are not in right now.* **Ahorita las faldas largas no están de moda.**

to be in a tight spot —**Estar en aprietos; estar en dificultades**

to be in apple pie order —**Estar como Dios manda; estar perfectamente ordenado(a)**

to be in charge of (something) —**Estar a cargo de (algo)**

to be in deep water —**Estar en aprietos; estar en dificultades**

to be in the limelight —**Ser el centro de atracción (atención)**

to be in the/(someone's) way —**Estorbar** ▪ *That chair is in the way.* **Esa silla estorba. (Esa silla está estorbando.)** *Move. You're in my way.* **¡Quítate, me estás estorbado!**

to be in your best bib and tucker —**Estar con sus mejores galas; estar emperifollado(a);** *(Arg)* **estar muy currutaco(a)**

to be in your birthday suit —**Estar desnudo(a); estar como Dios lo(a) trajo al mundo** (*lit.* to be as God brought you into this world)

to be jet black —**Ser negro azabache**

to be left holding the bag —**Tener que cargar con el muerto** (*lit.* to have to dispose of the corpse) ▪ *Guess who was left holding the bag.* **Adivina quién tuvo que cargar con el muerto.**

to be made the scapegoat —**Ser el chivo expiatorio; pagar los platos rotos** ▪ *I think I'm going to be made the scapegoat.* **Creo que voy a tener que pagar los platos rotos.**

to be madly in love —**Estar locamente (perdidamente) enamorado(a)**

to be mean —**Ser una mula**

to be not half bad —**No estar (nada) mal** ▪ *Try the cake. It's not half bad.* **Prueba el pastel. No está mal.**

to be nuts —**Estar demente; estar loco(a);** (slang) **patinar(le) el coco**

to be on a first-name basis —**Tutear(se)** ▪ *How long have you been on a first-name basis?* **¿Desde cuándo se tutean ustedes?**

to be on duty —**Estar de guardia; estar de turno**

to be on the ball —**Poner(se) vivo(a); poner(se) alerta** ▪ *You've got to be on the ball.* **Hay que ponerse vivo.**

to be on the go —**Andar a la carrera** (*lit.* to be racing around)

---

to be on the level —**Hablar en serio**

to be on the spot —**Estar en aprietos; estar en dificultades**

to be on your last legs —**Estar en las últimas** ▪ *Poor horse! It's on its last legs.* **¡Pobre caballo! Está en las últimas.**

to be on your toes —**Poner(se) vivo(a); poner(se) alerta; poner(se) abusado(a)**

to be on your way —**Estar en camino**

to be out of (something) —**Ya no tener; ya no haber** ▪ *I'm out of money.* **Ya no tengo dinero.** *We're out of time.* **Ya no tenemos tiempo.**

to be out of order —**Estar descompuesto(a); no servir** ▪ *The phone is out of order.* **El teléfono está descompuesto (no sirve).**

to be out of your mind —**Estar demente; estar loco(a)**

to be over —**Acabar(se); terminar(se)** ▪ *The meeting is over.* **Terminó la junta.**

to be (way) overdressed —*(Mex)* **Colgar(se) hasta el molcajete (la mano del metate)**

to be peculiar —**Ser raro;** (slang) **ser (un) bicho raro** (*lit.* to be a strange bug); **ser especial** ▪ *Don't tell me the new accountant isn't a bit peculiar.* **No me digas que el nuevo contador no es raro (un bicho raro) (muy especial).**

to be plastered —**Estar tomado(a); estar borracho(a); estar cuete;** *(Gua)* **estar bolo(a);** *(Arg)* **traer una buena mamúa**

to be saddled with —**Tener que cargar con** ▪ *Poor Thurston is saddled with that dreadful debt.* **El pobre de Thurston tiene que cargar con esa enorme deuda.**

to be second to none —**No tener rival** ▪ *This tequila is second to none.* **Este tequila no tiene rival.**

to be snotty —**Ser creído(a); dar(selas) de importante; dar(selas) de (algo)** ▪ *The boss's daughter is really snotty.* **La hija del jefe es muy creída (se las da de importante).**

to be starved —**Estar muerto(a) de hambre**

to be starving —**Estar muriéndose de hambre**

to be stingy —**Ser tacaño(a); ser avaro(a);** *(Mex)* **ser pichicato(a);** *(Ven)* **ser pichirre;** *(Arg)* **ser amarrete**

to be stuck —**Estar atorado(a)** ▪ *We were stuck in the elevator for half an hour.* **Estuvimos atorados en el elevador durante media hora.**

to be sunk —**Estar perdido(a); estar en la olla**

to be supposed to (+ verb) —**Se supone que debe** (+ verb) (**suponer** and **deber** are both conjugated) ▪ *We're supposed to be there now. Se supone que ya debiéramos estar ahí.*

to be taken in —**Ser engañado(a)** ▪ *I was completely taken in by his letter of recommendation.* **Me engañaron por completo con su carta de recomendación.**

to be the apple of (someone's) eye —**Ser la niña de los ojos de (alguien)**

to be the black sheep of the family —**Ser la oveja negra de la familia**

to be the last straw —**Ser la gota que derramó el vaso** (*lit.* to be the drop that overflowed the glass)

to be tickled pink —**Estar encantado(a); estar fascinado(a); estar feliz de la vida**

to be tickled to death —**Estar encantado(a); estar fascinado(a); estar feliz de la vida**

to be tight —**Estar mareado(a); andar (estar) borracho(a);** *(Gua)* **estar bolo(a)**

to be tipsy —**Estar mareado(a); andar (estar) borracho(a);** *(Gua)* **estar bolo(a)**

to be too big for your britches —**Subir(sele) los humos a la cabeza** ▪ *That fellow is too big for his britches.* **A ese tipo se le subieron los humos a la cabeza.**

to be touchy —**Ser sentido(a)** ▪ *Don't tease Pablo too much. He's very touchy.* **No vaciles mucho a Pablo. Es muy sentido.**

to be unable to put up with (someone or something) —**No tolerar a (alguien o algo); no soportar a (alguien o algo); no aguantar a (alguien o algo)** ▪ *I can't put up with that woman.* **No tolero (soporto, aguanto) a esa mujer.**

to be unable to stand (someone or something) —**No tolerar a (alguien o algo); no soportar a (alguien o algo); no aguantar a (alguien o algo)**

to be under the weather —**Sentir(se) mal; no sentir(se) bien**

to be unhinged —**Estar loco(a), tocado(a), zafado(a);** (slang) **hacer(le) falta un tornillo**

to be up and about —**Estar levantado(a)** (in the morning)**; ya no estar en cama** (after an illness/operation)

---

to be up to (someone) —**Ser decisión de (alguien)** ▪ *The color is up to you.* **El color es tu decisión. (Tú decides el color.)**

to be up to here —**Estar harto(a); estar hasta la coronilla;** *(Arg)* **estar podrido**

to be used to —**Estar acostumbrado(a) a** ▪ I'm not used to eating chili. **No estoy acostumbrada a comer chile.** *I'm not used to this food.* **No estoy acostumbrada a esta comida.**

to be very bright —**Ser muy listo(a); ser muy vivo(a)**

to be worn out (very tired) —**Estar exhausto(a), muerto(a), agotado(a), rendido(a);** *(Mex)* **poner(se) una soba;** *(Arg)* **estar amasijado(a)** ▪ *I'm worn out.* **Estoy exhausto (muerto) (agotado) (rendido) (amasijado). (Me puse una soba.)**

to be worth (+ verb) —**Valer la pena** (+ verb) ▪ *It's not worth going all that way.* **No vale la pena ir hasta allá.**

to be worth it —**Valer la pena** ▪ *It's not worth it.* **No vale la pena.**

to beat around the bush —**Andar(se) con rodeos** ▪ *Don't beat around the bush.* **No te andes con rodeos.**

to beat (someone) hands down —**Ganar (le) a (alguien) de todas, todas**

better half —**Media naranja**

Better not. —**Mejor no.**

(The) big shot —**El mandamás**

to bite (someone's) head off —**Regañar severamente a (alguien); gritar(le) a (alguien); poner(le) una regañiza a (alguien)** ▪ *Armando bit off my head!* **Armando me puso una regañiza (me gritó) (me regañó severamente).**

to bite off more than you can chew —**Meter(se) en camisa de once varas** ▪ *I think Burt bit off more than he can chew.* **Creo que Burt se metió en camisa de once varas.**

to blow (something) —1) **Malgastar;** (slang) **tronar(se) (dinero)** (To blow (money)) ▪ *Jorge blew his whole salary payment at the gambling table.* **Jorge malgastó (se tronó) toda su quincena apostando.** —2) **Echar a perder (algo)** (to screw (something) up) ▪ *That nitwit blew the negotiations with the bank.* **Ese tarado echó a perder la negociación con el banco.**

to blow it —**Equivocar(se);** (slang) **meter la pata** (*lit.* to stick your foot in it); *(Mex)* **regar(la)** (*lit.* to spill it) ▪ *I blew it!* **Me equivoqué. (Metí la pata.) (La regué.)**

to blow off steam —**Desahogar(se)**

to blow (one's) own horn —**Alabar(se) a sí mismo; echar(se) flores;** *(Mex)* (slang) **echar(se) guayabazos;** *(Ven)* **dar(se) bomba** ▪ *Gaston is never embarrassed to blow his own horn.* **A Gastón no le da pena echarse flores (echarse guayabazos) (alabarse a sí mismo).**

to blow your top —**Enojar(se); sulfurar(se); hacer un tango; hacer un drama** ▪ *You blow your top just because of that?* **¿Te enojas (te sulfuras; haces un tango; haces un drama) nada más por eso?**

to boot (someone) out —*(Mex)* (slang) **Correr a (alguien); poner de patitas en la calle a (alguien)** ▪ *Her father booted him out.* **Su papá lo corrió (lo puso de patitas en la calle).**

to break down —**Descomponer(se);** *(Mex)* (slang) **desconchinflar(se)** ▪ *The copier broke down.* **La copiadora se descompuso (se desconchinfló).**

to break the ice —**Romper el hielo**

to bring home the bacon —**Sacar para el gasto** ▪ *How am I going to bring home the bacon?* **¿Cómo voy a sacar para el gasto?**

to brownnose —*(Mex)* (slang) **Hacer(le) la barba a (alguien)**

to bug —**Molestar;** (vulgar) **fregar;** *(Mex)* (slang) **enchinchar** ▪ *Stop bugging me!* **¡No me estés molestando (fregando; enchinchando)!**

Bull! —**¡Esas son tonterías!; ¡Esas son mentiras!; ¡No me engañas!;** (slang) **¡No quieras tomarme el pelo!**

to burn the candle at both ends —**Buscar(se) un problema**

to burn your bridges behind you —**Quemar sus naves** (*lit.* to burn your ships)

to bury the hatchet —**Hacer las paces**

to bury your head in the sand —**Cerrar los ojos a (Negar) la realidad; esconder la cabeza; hacer lo que el avestruz**

to (nearly) bust a gut —**Casi sacar(se) una hernia** ▪ *I had to push the car all the way here. I nearly busted a gut.* **Tuve que empujar el coche hasta aquí. Casi me saco una hernia.**

to buy a pig in a poke —**Comprar a ciegas; comprar (algo) a lo tonto; comprar algo sin saber lo que se hace**

by leaps and bounds —**A pasos agigantados** ▪ *The group is gaining popularity by leaps and bounds.* **El grupo va ganando popularidad a pasos agigantados.**

by myself, yourself, etc. —**Solo(a); solito(a)** ▪ *I did it by myself.* **Lo hice yo solo (solito).**

---

by the skin of your teeth —(slang) **Por un pelito** (*lit.* by a little hair); **por un pelo de rana** (*lit.* by a frog's hair) ▪ *He passed the test by the skin of his teeth.* ***Aprobó el examen por un pelito de rana.***

by the way —**Por cierto; a propósito** ▪ *I was visiting my brother. By the way, he sends his regards.* ***Estuve de visita con mi hermano. Por cierto, te manda saludar.*** *The mail just arrived. By the way, there are two letters for you.* ***Acaba de llegar el correo. A propósito, hay dos cartas para ti.***

C

to call a spade a spade —**Llamar(le) al pan pan, y al vino vino**

to call (someone) all the names in the book —**Insultar a (alguien)**

to call (something) off —**Cancelar (algo)**

to call the shots —**Dar las órdenes**

to carry out —**Efectuar; llevar a cabo** ▪ *The study will be carried out in May.* **El estudio se efectuará (se llevará a cabo) en mayo.**

to change your mind —**Cambiar de parecer; cambiar de idea; cambiar de opinión** ▪ *Please don't change your mind again.* **Por favor, no vuelvas a cambiar de parecer.**

to cheer up —**Alegrar(se)** ▪ *Cheer up! Things aren't all that bad.* **¡Alégrate! Las cosas no están tan mal.**

to chill out —**Calmar(se);** *(Mex)* (slang) **no esponjar(se)** ▪ *Chill out!* **¡Cálmate! (¡No te esponjes!)**

a cock-and-bull story —**Un cuento chino** (*lit.* a Chinese story)

to come across —**Encontrar(se)** ▪ *I came across these letters in the attic.* **Me encontré estas cartas en el desván.**

come hell or high water —**Contra viento y marea; cueste lo que cueste; pase lo que pase** ▪ *I'm going to finish these two translations today, come hell or high water.* **Voy a terminar estas dos traducciones hoy, cueste lo que cueste (pase lo que pase).**

Come off it! —**¡Esas son tonterías!; ¡Esas son mentiras!; ¡No me engañas!;** (slang) **¡No quieras tomarme el pelo!**

to come on to (someone) —**Coquetear(le) a (alguien); insinuar(sele) a (alguien);** *(Mex)* (slang) **echar(le) los perros a (alguien)** ▪ *That guy came on to me at the party.* **Ese tipo se me estuvo insinuando (me echó los perros) (me estuvo echando los perros) en la fiesta.**

to come true —**Hacer(se) realidad** ▪ *I hope my dream will come true.* **Espero que mi sueño se haga realidad.**

to cook (someone's) goose —**Hacer que (alguien) pague el precio**

Cool! —**¡Sensacional!;** *(Mex)* (slang) **¡Qué padre!; ¡Padrísimo!; ¡Qué a todo dar!**

Cool it! —**¡Bájale¡; ¡Contrólate!; ¡Se te está pasando la mano!**

to cop out —**Echar(se) para atrás;** *(Mex)* **Rajar(se)** ▪ *Didn't I tell you he was going to cop out?* **¿No te dije que se iba a echar para atrás?**

to count on (someone or something) —**Contar con (alguien o algo);**

depender de (alguien o algo) ▪ *I know I can't count on Jack.* **Ya sé que no cuento con Jack.**

to crack up —**Reír(se) mucho; desternillar(se) de risa** ▪ *When John heard the story, he cracked up.* **Cuando John oyó la historia, se rió mucho (se desternilló de risa).**

to cut down on (something) —**Reducir (algo);** (slang) **bajar(le) a (algo)** ▪ *We have to cut down on all this spending.* **Tenemos que reducir los gastos. (Tenemos que bajarle a esta gastadera.)**

to (not) cut it —**No ser satisfactorio;** *(Mex)* (slang) **no hacer(la)** ▪ *This wine doesn't cut it.* **Este vino no la hace. (Este vino no es satisfactorio.)**

Cut it out! —**¡Basta!; !Párale!**

to cut (something) out —**Eliminar** ▪ *We'll have to cut out the side trip to Valparaíso.* **Tendremos que eliminar el viaje a Valparaíso.**

to dawn on —**Dar(se) cuenta; venir(le) una idea de pronto (o de repente); prender(sele) el foco** ▪ *It finally dawned on me who she was!* **¡Finalmente me di cuenta quién era ella!**

to die with your boots on —**Morir(se) con las botas puestas**

to dig your own grave —**Cavar su propia tumba**

to do a snow job —**Engañar a (alguien);** *(Mex)* (slang) **ver(le) la cara a (alguien)** ▪ *The guy at the shop did a snow job on me.* **El tipo del taller me engañó (me vio la cara).**

to do (something) by hook or by crook —**Lograr (algo) por las buenas o por las malas; lograr (algo) a como dé lugar** ▪ *I'm going to get into that club by hook or by crook!* **Voy a entrar a ese club a como dé lugar (por las buenas o por las malas).**

to do (something) over —**Repetir (algo); hacer de nuevo (algo)**

to do without (something) —**Prescindir de (algo)** ▪ *I really can't do without my glasses.* **Realmente no puedo prescindir de mis lentes.**

Don't panic! —**¡Que no cunda el pánico!**

Don't waste your breath! —**¡No pierdas tu tiempo!; ¡No gastes saliva!**

(a) double-edged sword —**Arma de dos filos** ▪ *Atomic energy is a double-edged sword.* **La energía atómica es un arma de dos filos.**

to draw up —**Formular; preparar; redactar** ▪ *The lawyers are drawing up the agreement.* **Los abogados están formulando (preparando; redactando) el contrato.**

to dress to kill —**Ir con su mejor ropa; ir emperifollado(a); emperifollar(se);** *(Arg)* **ir muy currutaco(a)** ▪ *They were all dressed to kill.* **Todos iban emperifollados (muy currutacos) (con su mejor ropa).**

to drive (someone) crazy (nuts) —**Volver loco(a) a (alguien)** ▪ *That noise is driving me crazy.* **Ese ruido me está volviendo loco.**

to drop (into bed) (from exhaustion) —(slang) **Caer como tabla** (*lit.* to fall like a board) ▪ *I fell into bed at ten last night.* **Caí como tabla anoche a las diez.**

Drop dead! —**¡Vete al diablo! (¡Váyanse al diablo!)**

to drop in on (someone) —**Dar(se) una vuelta;** (slang) **caer(le) a (alguien)** ▪ *I think I'll drop in on Gus tomorrow.* **Creo que mañana me voy a dar una vuelta por casa de Gustavo.**

to end up —**Terminar en** ▪ *We were only going to Cuernavaca, but ended up in Taxco.* **Sólo íbamos a Cuernavaca, pero terminamos en Taxco.**

to end up (+ verb + ing) —**Terminar** (+ verb + **ndo**) ▪ *Naturally, Dad ended up paying.* **Naturalmente, Papá terminó pagando.**

F

Face it! —¡Enfréntalo!; Enfrenta la realidad de las cosas.

(a) fair-weather friend —Amigo(a) sólo en las buenas; amigo(a) interesado

to fall behind —Atrasar(se) ▪ *We fell behind with the payments.* **Nos atrasamos con los pagos.**

to fall in love —Enamorar(se) de (alguien) ▪ *Looks like Marta is falling in love with Pablo.* **Parece que Marta se está enamorando de Pablo.**

to fall short of —No lograr el objetivo; quedar(se) corto(a) ▪ *We are falling short of the target.* **No estamos logrando el objetivo. (Nos estamos quedando cortos.)**

to fall through —No hacer(se); no lograr(se) ▪ *The projected trip fell through.* **El viaje proyectado no se hizo (no se logró; se canceló).**

to fall through the cracks —Desaparecer; tragar(selo) la tierra ▪ *Half the people who should have been at the 25-year reunion have just fallen through the cracks.* **Nadie sabe nada de la mitad de la gente que debía estar en la reunión del 25 aniversario. Parece que se los tragó la tierra. (Desaparecieron.)**

to feel (something) in your bones —Tener el presentimiento; tener una corazonada; *(Mex)* (slang) latir(le) (algo a alguien) ▪ *Bruce is going to dump me. I feel it in my bones.* **Me late que Bruce me va a dejar.**

to feel like (something) —Tener ganas de (algo) ▪ *I feel like a big ice cream.* **Tengo ganas de un heladote.**

to feel like (+ verb + ing) —Tener ganas de (+ infinitive verb) ▪ *I feel like going to Cancun this winter.* **Tengo ganas de ir a Cancún este invierno.**

to feel like a million dollars —Sentir(se) de maravilla (physically); sentir(se) realizado(a) (morally/emotionally) ▪ *A week of rest made me feel like a million dollars.* **Una semana de descanso me hizo sentirme de maravilla.** *I felt like a million dollars when they gave me the prize.* **Me sentí realizado cuando me dieron el premio.**

to feel sorry for (someone) —Sentir lástima por (alguien); sentir pena por (alguien); sentir(lo) por (alguien) ▪ *I feel sorry for her.* **Siento lástima por ella. (Lo siento por ella.)**

to fend for yourself —Arreglar(selas) solo(a); (slang) rascar(se) con sus propias uñas ▪ *He doesn't know how to shift for himself.* **No sabe arreglárselas solo. (No sabe rascarse con sus propias uñas.)**

few and far between —Escasos(as); contados(as) ▪ *Gas stations are few*

---

and far between in this area of Chiapas. **Hay contadas gasolineras en esta parte de Chiapas.**

to fight a losing battle —**Estar perdido(a) de antemano** ▪ *I feel I'm fighting a losing battle.* **Siento que este asunto está perdido de antemano.**

to fight tooth and nail —**Defender(se) hasta con los dientes; defender(se) como gato boca arriba** ▪ *She fought tooth and nail.* **Se defendió como gato boca arriba.**

to figure (someone or something) out —**Encontrar(le) sentido a (algo); entender(le) a (alguien o algo); explicar(se) (algo)** ▪ *I can't figure out her writing.* **No le entiendo a su letra.** *I can't figure out how this works.* **No me explico cómo funciona esto.**

to figure out how to ... —**Encontrar la manera de ...; ingeniar (selas) para ...** ▪ *You have to figure out how to pay back that money.* **Tienen que encontrar la manera de pagar esa deuda. (Van a tener que ingeniárselas para pagar esa deuda.)** *I have to figure out how to make this work.* **Tengo que ingeniármelas para hacer que esto funcione.**

to fill (something) out —**Llenar (algo)** ▪ *Please fill out the application.* **Llene la solicitud, por favor.**

to fill the bill —**Servir; dar el ancho; ser lo que se necesita; cumplir con los requisitos** ▪ *This applicant really fills the bill.* **Este candidato sí que da el ancho.**

to find out —**Averiguar; investigar** ▪ *Please find out who did this.* **Por favor averigua quién hizo esto.**

first of all... —**Primero que nada...; antes que nada...; antes que otra cosa...**

a flash in the pan —*(Mex)* **Llamarada de petate**

to fly off the handle —**Perder los estribos** (*lit.* to lose your stirrups) ▪ *He flew off the handle when I told him about the car.* **Perdió los estribos cuando le dije lo del coche.**

to fool (someone) —**Engañar a (alguien); defraudar a (alguien)**

to fool around —**Echar relajo** ▪ *Jimmy is fooling around with the dog.* **Jimmy está echando relajo con el perro.**

for a change —**Para variar** ▪ *We're going to stay home for Christmas this year, for a change.* **Este año nos vamos a quedar en casa para la Navidad, para variar.**

for good —**Para siempre** ▪ *He's leaving for good.* **Se va para siempre.**

for the time being —**Por el momento; por ahora; mientras tanto;**

entre tanto; por mientras ▪ *There's no danger, for the time being.* ***Por el momento, no hay peligro.*** *We can use this space for the time being.* ***Podemos usar este espacio mientras tanto.***

to fork out the dough —**Pagar;** *(Mex)* **caer(se) con la lana** ▪ *I don't want any excuses. Fork out the dough!* ***No quiero excusas. ¡Cáete con la lana!***

to fork out the money —**Pagar**

to freak out —**Poner(se) histérico(a); infartar(se);** (slang) **dar(le) el soponcio** ▪ *Don't show Jennifer that spider. She'll freak out.* ***No le enseñes esa araña a Jennifer. Se va a poner histérica. (Se va a infartar.) (Le va a dar el soponcio.)***

from the get-go —**Desde el principio**

to get along in years —**Envejecer**

to get along on a shoestring —**Vivir con muy poco dinero**

to get along with (someone) —**Llevar(se) (bien) (con alguien)** ▪ *Pepe and I get along fine, but I don't get along with Andrés.* **Pepe y yo nos llevamos muy bien, pero no me llevo con Andrés.**

to get all dolled up —**Emperifollar(se)** ▪ *She got all dolled up for the party.* **Se emperifolló para la fiesta.**

to get away with (something) —**Salir(se) con la suya (tuya)** ▪ *You're not going to get away with this.* **No te vas a salir con la tuya.**

to get back at (someone) —**Desquitar(se) de (alguien); vengar(se) de (alguien)** ▪ *I know how I'm going to get back at him!* **¡Ya sé como me voy a desquitar (vengar) de él!**

to get blood out of a stone —**Sacar agua de las piedras**

to get carried away —**Alocar(se);** (slang) **pasar(sele) la mano;** *(Mex)* **acelerar(se)** ▪ *I got carried away and bought the whole set.* **Se me pasó la mano (me aloqué; me aceleré) y compré todo el juego.**

to get going —(slang) **Arrancar(se)** ▪ *Well, get going with the report.* **Bueno, arráncate con el informe.**

to get hooked on (something) —**Enamorar(se) de (algo); fascinar(se) con (algo)** (when referring to alcohol, cigarettes, drugs, etc., use **ser adicto a**) ▪ *Lorenzo is getting hooked on scuba diving.* **Lorenzo está fascinado con el buceo.**

to get hot under the collar —**Enfurecer(se); sulfurar(se); enfadar(se); molestar(se)** ▪ *I apologize. Don't get hot under the collar.* **Me disculpo. No te sulfures. (No te molestes.)**

to get in over your head —**Meter(se) en camisa de once varas** ▪ *I'm afraid John has gotten in over his head.* **Me temo que John se ha metido en camisa de once varas.**

to get in touch with (someone) —**Poner(se) en contacto con (alguien)** ▪ *I'll get in touch with you later.* **Más tarde me pondré en contacto contigo.**

to get (something) off the ground —**Poner en marcha (algo)** ▪ *It's taking forever to get this project off the ground.* **Nos estamos tardando demasiado en poner en marcha este proyecto.**

to get on your nerves —**Irritar; poner de mal humor a (alguien);** *(Mex)* **poner de malas a (alguien)** ▪ *That music gets on my nerves.* **Esa** *música me irrita (me pone de mal humor) (me pone de malas).*

to get out of hand —**Salir(se) de control**

to get out of line —**Hacer (algo) indebido;** *(Mex)* (slang) **salir(se) del huacal** (*lit.* to get out of the cage)

to get out the kinks —**Eliminar los problemas**

to get over (something) —1) **Reponer(se)** ▪ *I hope you get over that hepatitis soon.* **Espero que te repongas pronto de esa hepatitis.** —2) **No poder creer (algo)** ▪ *Ruth just can't get over Geoff's death.* **Ruth no puede creer que Geof haya muerto.**

to get rid of (something) —**Deshacer(se) de (algo)** ▪ *Get rid of that stuff, will you?* **Deshazte de esas cosas, por favor.**

to get riled up —**Enfurecer(se); encender(se); sulfurar(se);** *(Mex)* (slang) **esponjar(se)** ▪ *He gets riled up every time he sees me.* **Se enfurece cada vez que me ve.**

to get stuck —**Atorar(se)** ▪ *My zipper got stuck.* **Se me atoró el cierre.**

to get the hang of (something) —**Encontrar(le) el modo a (algo)** ▪ *I'm beginning to get the hang of these skates.* **Estoy empezando a encontrarle el modo a estos patines.**

to get the show on the road —**Echar a andar** (+ event)**; arrancar con** (+ event) ▪ *Let's get the show on the road!* **Vamos a echar a andar esta junta.**

to get too big for your boots —**Dejar que se le suban los humos a la cabeza**

to get up on the wrong side of the bed —**Levantar(se) con el pie izquierdo** (*lit.* to get up with your left foot)**; andar de malas**

to get used to —**Acostumbrar(se) a** ▪ *I have to get used to getting up early.* **Tengo que acostumbrarme a levantarme temprano.** *I have to get used to this weather.* **Tengo que acostumbrarme a este clima.**

to get with it —**Poner(se) vivo(a)**

to get your own back —**Desquitar(se); vengar(se)** ▪ *Did you see what that bastard did to me? I'm going to get mine. You'll see.* **¿Viste lo que me hizo ese desgraciado? Me voy a desquitar. Ya verás.**

to give (someone) a hand —**Dar(le) (echar(le)) una mano a (alguien)**

to give (someone) a hard time —**Cargar(le) la mano a (alguien)**

to give (someone) a piece of your mind —**Cantar(le) sus verdades a (alguien); regañar severamente a (alguien); gritar(le) a (alguien)** to give (someone) a ride —**Llevar a (alguien) (en el auto)**; *(Mex)* **dar(le) un aventón a (alguien)**

to give (someone) a ring —**Llamar (por teléfono) a (alguien)** ▪ *Give me a ring when you get home.* **Llámame cuando llegues.**

to give (someone) a taste of his own medicine —**Dar(le) una sopa de su propio chocolate a (alguien)** (*lit.* to give someone a soup of his own chocolate)

to give (someone or something) a wide berth —**Sacar(le) la vuelta a (alguien o algo)** ▪ *I always give that woman a wide berth. I don't want problems.* **Siempre le saco la vuelta a esa mujer. No quiero problemas.**

to give (someone) free rein —**Soltar(le) la rienda a (alguien); dar rienda suelta a (algo)** ▪ *I hope I didn't make a mistake by giving her free rein.* **Espero no haber cometido un error al soltarle la rienda.**

to give (someone) hell —**Regañar severamente a (alguien); gritar(le) a (alguien)** ▪ *Lilly gave me hell for forgetting the appointment.* **Lilly me puso una regañiza por olvidar la cita.**

Give him (her) an inch, and he'll (she'll) take a mile —**Le das la mano, y se toma hasta el pie (brazo)**

to give in —**Ceder a la voluntad de (alguien); aceptar cambiar de opinión;** (slang) **doblar las manos** ▪ *She was right, so I had to give in.* **Ella tenía razón, y tuve que aceptarlo (tuve que doblar las manos).**

Give it a rest! —**¡Ya basta!; ¡Ya párale! (¡Ya párenle!)**

Give me a break! —**¡Esas son tonterías!; ¡Esas son mentiras!; ¡No me engañas!;** (slang) **¡No quieras tomarme el pelo!**

to give (someone) the cold shoulder —**Volver(le) la espalda a (alguien)**

to give (someone) the shaft (to shaft; to get shafted) —**Hacer(le) una mala jugada a (alguien);** *(Mex)* (slang) **dar(le) en la torre a (alguien);** *(Mex)* (slang) **pasar a torcer a (alguien)** ▪ *The S.O.B. told Mary all about my affair with Tiffany. He really gave me the shaft.* **El tal por cual me hizo una mala jugada (me dio en la torre; me pasó a torcer). Le contó a Mary lo de mi aventura con Tiffany.**

to give (someone) the slip —**Escapar(sele) a (alguien);** *(Mex)* (slang) **pelar(sele) a (alguien)** ▪ *Where's Pepe? He gave me the slip.* **¿Dónde está Pepe? Se me peló (escapó).**

to give up (stop trying) —**Rendir(se); dar(se) (por vencido(a))** ▪ *I'm not going to try again. I give up!* **No lo voy a volver a intentar. ¡Me rindo! (¡Me doy!)**

to give up (+ verb) (stop a habit) —**Dejar de** (+ verb) ▪ *I absolutely have to stop smoking!* **¡Definitivamente tengo que dejar de fumar!**

to give (someone his) walking papers —**Despedir a (alguien); correr a (alguien);** (slang) **poner de patitas en la calle a (alguien)** ▪ *Elvin was given his walking papers today.* **Hoy corrieron a Elvin.**

to give (someone) what he's got coming to him —**Dar(le) una sopa de su propio chocolate a (alguien)** (*lit.* to give someone a soup of his own chocolate) ▪ *Wait till I get my hands on Pepe. I'm going to give him what he's got coming to him.* **Espera que encuentre a Pepe. Le voy a dar una sopa de su propio chocolate.**

to give (something) your all —**Meter(le) (echar(le)) ganas; echar(le) los kilos** ▪ *You can still win. Give it your all!* **Aún puedes ganar. ¡Echale ganas (los kilos)!**

to go against the grain —**Ir contra la corriente** (*lit.* to go against the current)

to go all out —**Echar (tirar) la casa por la ventana** ▪ *It's my only daughter's wedding. We're going to go all out!* **Es la boda de mi única hija. ¡Vamos a echar la casa por la ventana!**

to go around the bend —**Volver(se) loco(a)** ▪ *I think Jack is going around the bend.* **Creo que Jack se está volviendo loco.**

to go crazy —**Volver(se) loco(a)** ▪ *I sometimes think I'll go crazy.* **A veces creo que me voy a volver loco.**

Go fly a kite! —**¡Vete al diablo!; ¡Váyase al diablo!**

to go from bad to worse —**Ir de mal en peor** ▪ *Until Jane arrived, everything was going from bad to worse.* **Hasta que Jane llegó, todo iba de mal en peor.**

to go it alone —**Arreglar(selas) solo(a);** (slang) **rascar(se) con sus propias uñas** ▪ *Son, the time has come for you to go it alone.* **Hijo, llegó el momento de que te las arregles solo (de rascarte con tus propias uñas).**

to go jump in the lake —**Ir(se) al diablo; ir(se) al demonio** ▪ *I told him to go jump in the lake.* **Le dije que se fuera al diablo.**

to go nuts —**Volver(se) loco(a)**

to go on a binge —**Ir(se) de parranda; ir(se) de juerga** ▪ *He goes on a binge every payday.* **Se va de parranda cada quincena.**

to go on the wagon —**Dejar de tomar (beber)** ▪ *None for me please. I'm on the wagon.* **Nada para mí, gracias. Dejé de tomar por algún tiempo.**

to go over (something) —**Revisar (algo)** ▪ *Go over the letter before I sign* *it. Revisa la carta antes de que la firme.*

to (really) go to town —**Dar(se) vuelo; dar(se) gusto** ▪ *With all that money we can really go to town decorating the house.* **Con todo ese dinero podemos darnos vuelo (gusto) decorando la casa.**

to go under —**Hundir(se)** (*lit.* to sink)

to go with (something) —**Hacer juego con (algo); ir con (algo)** ▪ *My shoes don't go with my bag.* **Mis zapatos no van (no hacen juego) con mi bolsa.**

to goof off —**Haraganear; flojear** ▪ *Pete's goofing off again.* **Pete está haraganeando de nuevo.**

to grease (someone's) palm —**Sobornar a (alguien);** *(Mex)* **dar una mordida** ▪ *I refuse to grease this guy's palm.* **Me niego a sobornar (darle una mordida) a ese tipo.**

had better —**Más vale que; es mejor que** ▪ *You had better go.* ***Más vale que te vayas. (Es mejor que te vayas.)***

to hand (something) in —**Entregar (algo)** ▪ *When are you going to hand in that report?* ***¿Cuándo vas a entregar ese informe?***

to hang around —**Esperar; no ir(se)** ▪ *Hang around for a while, please.* ***Espérate un rato, por favor. (No te vayas, por favor.)***

to have a bone to pick with (someone) —**Tener cuentas pendientes con (alguien); tener un problema pendiente con (alguien)**

to have a chip on your shoulder —**Ser una persona desagradable;** (slang) **ser pesado(a);** *(Mex)* **ser sangrón (sangrona)** ▪ *I'm afraid John has a chip on his shoulder.* ***Me temo que John es muy pesado (un sangrón).***

to have a fit —**Hacer un tango** *(lit.* to sing or dance a tango*)*; **hacer un drama o dramón** *(lit.* to be very dramatic about something*)*; **dar(le) el infarto** *(lit.* to have a heart attack*)*; *(Mex)* **dar(le) un soponcio;** *(Mex)* (slang) **dar(le) el (un) patatús** ▪ *She had a fit.* ***Hizo un tango (drama). (Le dio un infarto (patatús; soponcio).)***

to (not) have a ghost of a chance —**No lograr(se) (algo) ni de chiste** ▪ *Poor Justin doesn't have a ghost of a chance with Laura.* ***El pobre de Justin ni de chiste va a lograr algo con Laura.***

to have a good time —**Divertir(se); pasar(la) bien** ▪ *We had a good time!* ***¡Nos divertimos mucho! (¡La pasamos muy bien!)***

to have a green thumb —**Tener el don de la jardinería; tener buena mano para las plantas**

to have a hunch —**Tener el presentimiento; tener una corazonada;** *(Mex)* (slang) **latir(le) (algo)** ▪ *I have a hunch Pancho is going to win the contest.* ***Tengo la corazonada de (me late) que Pancho va a ganar el concurso.***

to have a lot on the ball —**Ser muy listo(a); ser muy vivo(a)** ▪ *I like Ann. She has a lot of smarts.* ***Me cae bien Ann. Es muy lista (viva).***

to have a lump in your throat —**Tener un nudo en la garganta**

to have a screw loose — **Estar loco(a), tocado(a), zafado(a);** (slang) **hacer(le) falta un tornillo; patinar(le) el coco** ▪ *I think the teacher has a screw loose.* ***Se me hace que el maestro está loco (al maestro le patina el coco).***

to have a soft spot for (something) —**Tener predilección por (algo); estar encariñado(a) con (algo)** ▪ *I have a soft spot for this cat.* ***Tengo*** *predilección por (estoy encariñado con) este gato.*

to have a voice in —**Tener vela en este entierro** (*lit.* to have a candle in this burial) ▪ *Shut up! You have no voice in this matter.* **¡Cállate! Tú no tienes vela en este entierro.**

to have an ax to grind —**Tener cuentas pendientes (con alguien); tener un problema pendiente (con alguien)**

to have bats in the belfry —**Estar demente; estar loco**

to have (something) done —**Mandar hacer (algo)** ▪ *I'm going to have the car fixed.* **Voy a mandar arreglar el coche.**

to have enough (something) to sink a ship —**Tener (algo) para aventar para arriba** ▪ *We have enough work to sink a ship.* **Tenemos trabajo para aventar para arriba.**

to have (someone) figured out —(slang) **Tener fichado(a) a (alguien)** ▪ *I've got you all figured out. I know just how you're going to react.* **Te tengo fichado, ya sé cómo vas a reaccionar.**

to have (something) figured out —**Tener todo resuelto; tener todo calculado**

to have guts —**Tener el valor**

to have irons in the fire —**Estar dándole vueltas a (algo)**

to have no choice —**No tener alternativa; (slang) no quedar de otra** ▪ *You have to get married. You have no choice!* **Te tienes que casar. ¡No te queda de otra!**

to have (someone's) number —(slang) **Tener fichado a (alguien)**

to have one too many —(slang) **Pasar(sele) las cucharadas** (*lit.* to have had too many spoonfuls) ▪ *Ted has had one too many.* **A Ted se le pasaron las cucharadas.**

to have (something) on the back burner —**Estar en veremos** (*lit.* to be in "we'll see" status) ▪ *The trip to Europe is on the back burner.* **El viaje a Europa está en veremos.**

to have (something) on your mind —**Estar preocupado(a) por (algo)**

to have spunk —**Tener mucho espíritu, fortaleza de carácter, empuje; (slang) ser entrón (entrona)** ▪ *He has got ahead because he has lots of spunk.* **Ha sobresalido porque tiene mucho espíritu (empuje; fortaleza de carácter) (porque es muy entrón).**

to have (something) to do with (someone or something) —**Tener (algo) que ver con (alguien o algo)** ▪ *What does that have to do with me?* **¿Eso qué tiene que ver conmigo?**

to have the gift of gab —**Tener labia** ▪ *I like your friend. She has the gift of gab.* **Me cae bien tu amiga. Tiene mucha labia.**

to have your hands full with (something) —**Tener mucho trabajo; tener un paquete con (algo)** ▪ *I really have my hands full with all these guests.* **De veras que tengo un paquete con todos estos invitados.**

to have your heart in the right place —**Tener buenos sentimientos**

He (She) doesn't eat enough to feed a bird. —**Come como pajarito.**

He's every inch a man. —**Es un hombre hecho y derecho.**

to hear from (someone) —**Saber de (alguien)** ▪ *What have you heard from Francis?* **¿Qué has sabido de Francis?**

to help yourself —**Servir(se)** (food); **¡Adelante!** (things other than food) ▪ *It's a buffet lunch. Help yourself.* **Hoy la comida es bufet. ¡Sírvete! (¡Sírvanse!)** *The books are over there. Help yourself.* **Los libros están allá. ¡Adelante!**

to hit pay dirt —**Tener suerte logrando un beneficio; sacar(se) la lotería** (literally or figuratively)

to hit the ceiling —**Colgar(se) de la lámpara** (*lit.* to leap onto the chandelier); **poner el grito en el cielo** (*lit.* to scream up into the sky); **parar(se) de pestañas** (*lit.* to stand on your eyelashes) ▪ *Wait till the boss sees this. He's going to hit the ceiling!* **Espera a que el jefe vea esto. ¡Se va a colgar de la lámpara! (¡Va a poner el grito en el cielo!) (¡Se va a parar de pestañas!)**

to hit the hay —**Ir(se) a la cama; acostar(se)**

to hit the nail on the head —**Dar en el clavo**

to hit the sack —**Ir(se) a la cama; acostar(se)**

to hold the fort —**Atender algo; encargar(se) de algo;** *(Mex)* **encargar(se) del changarro** ▪ *Hold the fort. I'll be back in a minute.* **Encárgate del changarro. Ahorita regreso.**

to hold up (a person or an establishment) —**Asaltar (algo o alguien)** (from an amateur stickup to a full-scale bank robbery) ▪ *I was held up last night.* **Anoche me asaltaron.**

Hold your horses! —**¡No te aceleres!; ¡Con calma y nos amanecemos!; ¡Momento de calma y la patria se salva!**

to horse around —**Echar relajo** ▪ *Those two are always horsing around.* **Esos dos siempre están echando relajo.**

hot air —**Tonterías; sandeces** ▪ *You're talking a lot of hot air.* **Estás diciendo puras tonterías (sandeces).**

h

How awful! —¡Qué espantoso!; ¡Qué horror!; ¡Qué horrible!

How come? —¿Y eso?

How ya doing? —¿Cómo te va?

to hush (something) up —Dar carpetazo a (algo); echar tierra al asunto a (algo); *(ES)* engavetar (algo) ▪ *This has to be hushed up. A esto hay que darle carpetazo (echarle tierra).*

I am all worn out! —(slang) **¡Estoy con la lengua de corbata!**

I can dream, can't I? —**Soñar no cuesta nada.**

I don't buy that! —**¡Eso no lo creo!; ¡Eso no me lo trago!**

I don't care! —**¡No me importa!; ¡Qué me importa!;** (slang) **¡Me vale!;** *(ES)* **¡Me vale riata!**

I just can't get over it! —**¡No lo puedo creer!**

I love it! —**¡Me encanta!**

I mean it! —**¡Lo digo en serio!**

I (you, he, etc.) missed the boat. —**Se me (te, le, etc.) fue este tren**

I want nothing to do with it! —**¡No me metas!; ¡No quiero saber nada del asunto!; ¡No quiero tener nada que ver con el asunto!**

I wouldn't dream of it! —**¡Ni soñarlo!**

I wouldn't touch it with a ten-foot pole! —**¡No quiero saber nada del asunto!**

in a hurry —**Aprisa; apresuradamente** ▪ *Pack your bags in a hurry.* **Haz las maletas aprisa.**

in a nutshell —**En pocas palabras** ▪ *That's the idea, in a nutshell.* **Esa es la idea, en pocas palabras.**

in every nook and cranny —**Por todos los rincones** ▪ *There were books and papers in every nook and cranny of his house.* **Había libros y papeles por todos los rincones de su casa.**

in fact —**De hecho; es más** ▪ *Yes, Dianne is a good friend. In fact, she's the best friend I've got.* **Sí, Dianne es buena amiga. Es más, es la mejor amiga que tengo.**

in the long run —**A larga; con el tiempo**

in the meantime —**Mientras; mientras tanto** ▪ *My computer is being fixed. In the meantime, I'm using this one.* **Están arreglando mi computadora. Mientras (mientras tanto), estoy usando ésta.**

in the nick of time —**Apenas a tiempo** ▪ *He grabbed the baby in the nick of time.* **Agarró al bebé apenas a tiempo.**

in the wee hours of the morning —**A altas horas de la madrugada; a las mil quinientas** ▪ *We finished in the wee hours of the morning.* **Terminamos a las mil quinientas.**

in this neck of the woods —**Por estos rumbos** ▪ *There are few drugstores*

---

in this neck of the woods. **Hay pocas farmacias por estos rumbos.**

inside out —**Al revés** ■ *The sweater is inside out.* **El suéter está al revés.**

Is that a threat or a promise? —**¿Es promesa o amenaza?**

It beats me! —**¡Ni idea!**

It doesn't ring a bell. —**No me suena.**

It figures. —**Tiene sentido.**

It makes no difference. —**No importa; Es lo mismo.**

It makes sense. —**Tiene sentido.**

It rings a bell. —**Me suena.**

Is that too much to ask? —**¿Es mucho pedir?**

It was a slip of the tongue. —**Lo dijo sin querer; Se le fue la lengua.**

It'll do. —**Esto servirá.**

It'll have to do. —**Esto tendrá que servir.**

It's a stone's throw from here. —**Está a tiro de piedra de aquí.**

It's about time! —**¡Ya era hora!**

It's better than nothing. —**Es mejor que nada; Peor es nada.**

It's like looking for a needle in a haystack. —**Es como buscar una aguja en un pajar.**

It's lovely! —**¡Es encantador(a)!**

It's my (your, his, etc.) turn! —**¡Me (te, le, etc.) toca!**

It's none of your business! —Formal: **No es de tu (su) incumbencia;** Familiar: **No te importa; ¿Qué te importa?**

It's not all fun and games. —**No todo es miel sobre hojuelas.**

It's out of the question. —**¡Imposible!; ¡Ni de chiste!; ¡Está fuera de discusión!**

It's raining cats and dogs! —**Está diluviando; Está lloviendo a cántaros.**

It's too much to ask! —**¡Es mucho pedir!**

I've (you've, he's, etc.) been had! —**¡Me (te, le, etc.) engañaron!;** *(Mex)* (slang) **¡Me (te, le, etc.) vieron la cara!**

J

(a) jalopy —**Carcacha**

to jump down (someone's) throat —**Regañar severamente a (alguien); gritar(le) a (alguien)** ▪ *He jumped down my throat.* **Me gritó (me regañó).**

to jump out of the frying pan into the fire —**Huir del fuego para caer en las brasas; salir de ansias para entrar en congojas; salir de Guatemala para entrar en Guatepeor**

to jump to conclusions —**Juzgar a la ligera; sacar conclusiones falsas**

just in case —**Por si (+ verb); por si acaso; por (si) las dudas** ▪ *Take an umbrella, just in case.* **Lleva paraguas, por si acaso.**

K

to keep a stiff upper lip —**Conservar la compostura**

to keep an eye on (something) —**Vigilar (algo);** *(Mex)* (slang) **echar(le) un ojo a (algo)** ▪ *Keep an eye on the kids.* **Echale un ojo a los niños. (Vigila a los niños.)**

to keep (someone) at arm's length —**Mantener a prudente distancia a (alguien)**

Keep quiet! —**¡Cállate! (¡Cállese!; ¡Cállense!)**

to keep the ball rolling —**Hacer algo para que no se muera (apague) (el interés por) (algo); hacer (algo) para que no se pierda el ritmo** ▪ *We've run out of whiskey. How are we going to keep the ball rolling?* **Se nos acabó el whisky. ¿Cómo le vamos a hacer para que no se apague la reunión?**

to keep track of (something) —**Llevar la(s) cuenta(s) de (algo)** ▪ *Are you keeping track of Peter's absences this month?* **¿Estás llevando la cuenta de las faltas (ausencias) de Peter de este mes?**

to keep up with (something) —**Seguir(le) el paso a (alguien)** ▪ *She can't keep up with my dictation.* **No me puede seguir el paso con el dictado.**

Keep your shirt on! —**¡Con calma y nos amanecemos!; ¡Momento de calma y la patria se salva!**

to kick ass —**Poner el orden; poner(se) enérgico(a);** (slang) **tronar el chicote** ▪ *If things aren't done the way I say, I'm going to have to kick* *some ass.* **Si las cosas no se hacen como yo digo, voy a tener que poner el orden (ponerme enérgico; tronarles el chicote).**

to kick (someone) out (off) —**Correr a (alguien); sacar a (alguien);** (slang) **poner de patitas en la calle a (alguien)** ▪ *My father kicked him out.* **Mi papá lo puso de patitas en la calle.**

to kick the bucket —**Morir(se); fallecer;** (slang) **estirar la pata;** *(Mex)* (slang) **colgar los tenis; petatear(se)** ▪ *He died. Murió. (Estiró la pata.) (Colgó los tenis.) (Se petateó.)*

to kill the goose that laid the golden eggs —**Matar la gallina de los huevos de oro**

to kill two birds with one stone —**Matar dos pájaros de un tiro (de una pedrada)**

Knock it off! —**¡Ya basta!; ¡Ya párale! (¡Ya párele; ¡Ya párenle!)**

to knock yourself out —**Matar(se) trabajando** ▪ *I knocked myself out getting ready for the party.* **Me maté haciendo los preparativos para la fiesta.**

to know (something) by heart —**Saber(se) (algo) de memoria** ▪ *I know the song by heart.* **Me sé la canción de memoria.**

to know the ropes —**Conocer el tejemaneje** ▪ *Go with Joe. He knows the ropes.* **Ve con Joe. El conoce el tejemaneje.**

to know which side his/her bread is buttered on —**Saber lo que le conviene** to lay down the law —**Leer(le) la cartilla a (alguien)** ▪ *He laid down the law on the first day.* **Nos leyó la cartilla el primer día.**

to lay off —**No acercar(se); mantener(se) lejos** ▪ *Remember, lay off the cake and ice cream.* **Recuerda… manténte lejos del pastel y del helado.**

Lay off! —**¡Ya basta!; ¡Ya párale! (¡Ya párele; ¡Ya párenle!)**

to lay people off —**Despedir; liquidar; correr** ▪ *The company laid off ten people this month.* **La empresa liquidó a diez personas este mes.**

to lead (someone) by the nose —**Tener dominado(a) a (alguien); traer marcando el paso a (alguien); traer cortito(a) a (alguien)** ▪ *Rose is leading her boyfriend around by the nose.* **Rose tiene dominado a su novio (trae marcando el paso a su novio; trae cortito a su novio).**

to leave a lot to be desired —**Dejar mucho que desear** ▪ *This leaves a lot to be desired.* **Esto deja mucho que desear.**

to leave (someone) breathless —**Dejar sin aliento a (alguien)**

to leave (something) out —**Omitir; olvidar incluir; no incluir** ▪ *Leave out the beer. We don't need it.* **Omite la cerveza. No la necesitamos.** *You accidentally left Gloria out.* **Se te olvidó incluir a Gloria.**

(a) left-handed compliment —**Un cumplido falso**

to let (someone) have it —**Decir(le) a (alguien) hasta la despedida; poner a (alguien) como camote** (verbally or physically)**; dar(le) una paliza a (alguien)** (to beat someone up) ▪ *When I tell Dad what you did, he's really going to let you have it.* **Cuando le diga a mi papá lo que hiciste, te va a dar una paliza (una regañiza) (te va a poner como camote).**

to let the cat out of the bag —**Revelar un secreto**

to let your arm be twisted —**Dar el brazo a torcer** ▪ *I'm not going to let my arm be twisted.* **No voy a dar el brazo a torcer.**

to let your hair down —**Sentir(se) en confianza**

to let yourself go —*(Mex)* **Afodongar(se); dejar(se); descuidar(se)** ▪ *After the divorce, she let herself go and got very fat.* **Después del divorcio se descuidó y se puso muy gorda.**

to lick your chops —**Saborear(se) (algo)** ▪ *Jim was licking his chops at the thought of a week in Cancún.* **Jim se saboreaba con la idea de una semana en Cancún.**

to (not) lift a finger —**No mover ni un dedo** ▪ *Amanda never lifts a finger around here.* **Amanda nunca mueve un dedo en esta casa.**

like a bat out of hell —**Como alma que lleva el diablo** (*lit.* like a soul taken by the devil) ▪ *He drives like a bat out of hell.* **Maneja como alma que lleva el diablo.**

Like it or lump it. —**Quiera(s) o no; le(te) guste o no** ▪ *This is what there is for breakfast, like it or lump it.* **Esto es lo que hay para desayunar, quieras o no.**

little by little —**Poco a poco** ▪ *Don't worry. You'll learn little by little.* **No te preocupes. Ya irás aprendiendo poco a poco.**

to live from hand to mouth —**Vivir al día**

to live it up —**Vivir con mucha alegría, plenamente; gozar la vida; saborear la vida**

(a) long face —**Cara larga** ▪ *Don't make a long face.* **No pongas cara larga.**

to look after (someone or something) —**Cuidar (alguien o algo)**

to look for trouble —**Buscar(se) un problema**

to look forward to (something) —**Esperar (algo) con ansias (entusiasmo); tener ganas de (algo) o de hacer (algo)** ▪ *I'm really looking forward to seeing Jonathan again.* **Espero con ansias volver a ver a Jonathan. (Tengo muchas ganas de volver a ver a Jonathan.)**

to look into (something) —**Investigar** ▪ *The police are looking into the suspect's record.* **La policía está investigando los antecedentes del sospechoso.**

Look out! —**¡Cuidado!;** *(Mex)* (slang) **¡Aguas!**

to look up —**Mejorar** ▪ *Things are looking up recently.* **Ultimamente las cosas están mejorando.**

to look (something) up —**Buscar**

to lose your cool —**Perder los estribos** (*lit.* to lose your stirrups) ▪ *When I mentioned Gretel, he lost his cool.* **Cuando mencioné a Gretel, perdió los estribos.**

to make a beeline for... —**Salir disparado(a) a (hacia)...** ▪ *She made a beeline for the bathroom.* **Salió disparada al (hacia el) baño.**

to make a boo-boo —**Equivocar(se); meter la pata** (*lit.* to stick your foot in it); *(Mex)* (slang) **regar(la)** (*lit.* to spill it) ▪ *You realize you made a boo-boo.* **Te das cuenta de que te equivocaste (metiste la pata) (la regaste).**

to make a mountain out of a molehill —**Hacer una tempestad en un vaso de agua**

to make ends meet —**Ganar lo suficiente;** (slang) **ir(la) librando** (aff.); **ir(la) pasando** (aff.); **no ganar lo suficiente** (neg.); **no alcanzar** (neg.); **no dar para todo** (neg.) ▪ *I'm more or less making ends meet.* **Más o menos la voy pasando (librando).**

to make fun of (someone or something) —**Burlar(se) de (alguien o algo)** ▪ *Don't make fun of his English.* **No te burles de su inglés.**

to make no sense —**No tener pies ni cabeza; no tener sentido** ▪ *That makes no sense.* **Eso no tiene sentido.**

to make sense —**Tener sentido** ▪ *That really makes sense.* **Eso sí tiene sentido.**

to make space for (something) —**Hacer campo (lugar, espacio) para (algo)**

to make sure —**Asegurar(se)** ▪ *Make sure there's gas in the car.* **Asegúrate de que el coche tenga gasolina.**

to make the best of a bad situation —**Al mal tiempo, buena cara** (a saying)

to make the most of (something) —**Aprovechar al máximo (algo); sacarle provecho a (algo)** ▪ *We have to make the most of this opportunity.* **Tenemos que aprovechar al máximo (sacarle provecho a) esta oportunidad.**

to make up (invent) (something) —**Inventar (algo)** ▪ *She made up a tall story.* **Inventó un cuento chino.**

to make up for (something) —**Compensar por (algo)** ▪ *I'll make up for this later, I promise.* **Te prometo que después te compenso por esto.**

to make up your mind —**Decidir(se)** ▪ *For heaven's sake, make up your mind!* **Por amor de Dios, ¡ya decídete!**

to make waves —**Hacer olas** ▪ *Just leave things as they are. Don't make waves.* **Dejen las cosas como están. No hagan olas.**

---

to make yourself scarce —**Esfumar(se); desaparecer;** *(Mex)* (slang) **pintarse (de colores); largar(se)** ▪ *Make yourself scarce.* ***¡Esfúmate! (¡Desaparece!; ¡Píntate de colores!; ¡Lárgate!)***

meanwhile —**Mientras; mientras tanto**

to meet (someone) (arriving on a trip) —**Recibir a (alguien)** ▪ *The whole family met me at the airport.* ***Toda la familia me recibió en el aeropuerto.***

to meet (someone's) match —**Encontrar (hallar) la horma de su zapato** ▪ *He finally met his match.* ***Hasta que encontró la horma de su zapato.***

to mess with (someone or something) —**Meter(se) con (alguien o algo)** ▪ *Don't mess with me!* ***¡No te metas conmigo!***

to mind the store —*(Mex)* **Encargar(se) del negocio; encargar(se) de la tienda; encargar(se) del changarro**

to monkey with (something) —**Meter(le) mano a (algo)** ▪ *Someone monkeyed with this engine.* ***Alguien le metió mano a este motor.***

more (something) than you can shake a stick at —**Para aventar para arriba** *(lit.* enough to fling up in the air) ▪ *That lady has more shoes than you can shake a stick at.* ***Esa señora tiene zapatos para aventar para arriba.***

Move over please. —**Hazte para allá, por favor. (Hágase para allá, por favor.)**

to mug (someone) —**Asaltar a (alguien)** ▪ *I was mugged.* ***Me asaltaron.***

My hands are tied. —**Estoy maniatado; No puedo hacer nada.**
▪ *I'm not her father, so my hands are tied.* ***No soy su padre, no puedo hacer nada (estoy maniatado).***

N

Never mind! —**¡Olvídalo!**

to nip (something) in the bud —**Cortar (acabar con) (algo) cuando empieza**

No sooner said than done. —**Dicho y hecho.**

No wonder! —**¡Con razón!**

not for love or money —**Ni a tiros; ni por todo el oro del mundo; por nada del mundo** ■ *I wouldn't go to live in China for love or money.* *No iría a vivir a China por nada del mundo.*

Not on your life! —**¡Ni de chiste!; ¡Ni loco!; ¡Ni de casualidad!;** (slang) **¡Ni con chochos!**

not yet —**Aún no; todavía no** ■ *I haven't finished yet.* *Todavía no termino.*

Now that I come to think of it... —**Ahora que lo pienso...**

null and void —**Sin efecto**

on purpose —**A propósito; adrede; intencionalmente**

On the double! —**¡Aprisa!**

on the other hand —**En cambio; por otra parte; por otro lado**

on the whole —**Por lo general; básicamente; en un alto porcentaje**

once and for all —**De una vez por todas** ▪ *Let's finish this job once and for all.* **Vamos a terminar este trabajo de una vez por todas.**

once in a blue moon —**Cada mil años** ▪ *David calls once in a blue moon.* **David llama cada mil años.**

once in a while —**De vez en cuando**

out of order —**Descompuesto(a)** ▪ *The telephone is out of order.* **El teléfono está descompuesto.**

out of print —**Agotado(a)** ▪ *I believe this book is out of print.* **Creo que este libro está agotado.**

out of stock —**Agotado(a)** ▪ *I am sorry. This CD is out of stock.* **Lo siento, este disco está agotado.**

out of the clear blue sky —**De buenas a primeras** ▪ *The band of dogs appeared out of the clear blue sky.* **La jauría apareció de buenas a primeras.**

out of thin air —**De la nada**

out of this world —**Fuera de serie; del otro mundo; fuera de este mundo** ▪ *This pie is out of this world!* **¡Este pastel está fuera de serie!**

over and over —**Una y otra vez**

over my dead body —**Sobre de mi cadáver** ▪ *You will marry that brute over my dead body!* **¡Te casas con esa bestia sobre mi cadáver!**

P

to pack your bags —**Hacer las maletas**

to pay lip service to (someone) —**Fingir estar de acuerdo con (alguien); decir (algo) de dientes para fuera**

to pay through the nose —**Pagar un precio exorbitante; pagar una fortuna** ▪ *I paid through the nose for this ring.* **Pagué una fortuna por este anillo.**

(A) penny for your thoughts. —**¿En qué piensas?**

to pick a quarrel —**Buscar pleito;** (slang) **buscar bronca;** *(Mex)* (slang) **buscar camorra; sacar boleto** ▪ *Please don't pick a quarrel.* **Por favor, no busques pleito (camorra; bronca).**

to pick up the tab —**Pagar la cuenta**

Pipe down! —**¡Cállate! (¡Cállense!);** (slang) **¡Bájale! (¡Bájenle!)**

to piss (someone) off —**Molestar a (alguien); enfurecer a (alguien)**

to play around —(slang) **Echar relajo**

to play ball —**Cooperar**

to play dead —**Hacer(se) el tonto (la tonta);** (slang) **hacer(se) el loco (la loca)** ▪ *Don't play dead!* **¡No te hagas el tonto (el muerto)!**

to play (something) down —**Minimizar (algo); no darle importancia a (algo)** ▪ *We played down the accident.* **No le dimos importancia al accidente.**

to play dumb —**Hacer(se) el tonto (la tonta);** (slang) **hacer(se) el loco (la loca)** ▪ *Don't play dumb!* **¡No te hagas el tonto (el loco)!**

to play hard to get —**Hacer(se) el/la interesante; hacer(se) el/la difícil** ▪ *She's playing hard to get.* **Se está haciendo la interesante.**

to play hooky —**Ir(se) de pinta** ▪ *They've played hooky twice this week.* **Se han ido de pinta dos veces esta semana.**

to play it cool —**Actuar como si nada (sucediera)** ▪ *She doesn't know about the accident. Play it cool.* **Ella no sabe lo del accidente. Actúa como si nada.**

to play it safe —**No arriesgar(se); no correr riesgo(s)** ▪ *It looks like it's going to rain. I'd better play it safe and just stay home.* **Parece que va a llover. Mejor no me arriesgo y me quedo en casa.**

to play the (anything) —**Dar(selas) de (algo)** ▪ *He likes to play the philanthropist.* **Le encanta dárselas de filántropo.**

to play the big shot —**Dar(selas) de importante** ▪ *He likes to play the* *big shot. **Le gusta dárselas de importante.***

to play the horses —**Apostar a las carreras de caballos**

to pop in on (someone) —**Dar(se) una vuelta;** (slang) **caer(le) a (alguien)** ▪ *I'm going to pop in on Nan.* **Me voy a dar una vuelta por casa de (caerle a) Nan.**

to pour oil on the fire —**Echar leña al fuego**

to promise the Earth —**Prometer el oro y el moro; prometer la luna y las estrellas**

to pull a fast one —**Engañar; defraudar** ▪ *I wouldn't be surprised if he tried to pull a fast one on Arturo.* **No me sorprendería que tratara de engañar a Arturo.**

to pull (someone's) leg —**Tomar(le) el pelo a (alguien)** (*lit.* to take someone's hair) ▪ *She's pulling your leg.* **Te está tomando el pelo.**

to pull (something) off —**Lograr (algo)** ▪ *It was difficult, but he pulled it off.* **Estaba en chino, pero lo logró.**

to pull strings —**Mover influencias;** (slang) **mover (usar) palancas** (*lit.* to move (to use) levers) ▪ *Can you pull strings to get me a building permit?* **Mueve tus palancas para conseguirme el permiso de construcción, ¿sí?**

to pull through —**Salir de un aprieto; aliviar(se)** (from an illness) ▪ *We'll pull through somehow.* **Saldremos del aprieto, de alguna manera.** *She'll pull through. The antibiotics are working.* **Se aliviará. Los antibióticos están haciendo efecto.**

to pull (something) to pieces —**Despedazar (algo); hacer pedazos (algo); hacer trizas (algo)** ▪ *The kid pulled the book to pieces.* **El niño despedazó (destrozó) (hizo pedazos) el libro.**

to pull your weight —**Hacer su parte; jalar parejo** ▪ *If you don't pull your weight, you're out.* **¡Si no haces tu parte (si no jalas parejo), te vas!**

to pull yourself together —**Controlar(se); calmar(se)**

to put in your two cents worth —**Meter su cuchara** ▪ *We don't need you to put in your two cents.* **No necesitamos que metas tu cuchara.**

to put (something) off —**Posponer (algo)**

to put the cart before the horse —**Adelantarse a los hechos** ▪ *You're putting the cart before the horse.* **Te estás adelantando a los hechos.**

to put the noose around your neck —**Poner(se) (echar(se)) la soga al cuello** ▪ *I'm afraid she put the noose around her neck.* **Me temo que se echó la soga al cuello.**

to put (something) together —**Armar (algo)** ■ *The instructions don't explain clearly how to put the toy together.* **El instructivo no explica con claridad cómo armar el juguete.**

to put up with (someone or something) —**Tolerar a (alguien o algo); aguantar a (alguien o algo)** ■ *I can't put up with that cheeky brat.* **No tolero (No aguanto) a ese niño malcriado.**

to put your foot in it; to put your foot in your mouth —**Equivocar(se);** (slang) **meter la pata** (*lit.* to stick your foot in it)**; regar(la)** (*lit.* to spill it) ■ *You put your foot in it again.* **Volviste a meter la pata. (La volviste a regar.)**

to put your nose to the grindstone —**Poner(se) a trabajar (estudiar)**

Quit it! —**¡Basta!; !Párale!**

quite a few —**Bastantes** ■ *We had quite a few complaints.* **Tuvimos bastantes quejas.**

R

rain or shine —**Llueva, truene o relampaguee** ▪ *He comes every Sunday, rain or shine.* **Viene todos los domingos, llueva, truene o relampaguee.**

to rave about (someone or something) —**Hablar maravillas de (alguien o algo)** ▪ *She's raving about the new house.* **Habla maravillas de la nueva casa.**

to reach a point of no return —**Llegar al punto en que ya no tiene remedio (algo); llegar a un punto en que ya no puede hacer(se) nada (hacer(se) para atrás)** ▪ *It looks as though we have reached a point of no return.* **Parece que hemos llegado al punto en que ya no podemos hacernos para atrás.**

to realize that (subject + verb) —**Dar(se) cuenta de que** (subject + verb) ▪ *I hadn't realized he has a glass eye.* **No me había dado cuenta de que tiene un ojo de vidrio.**

to rest on your laurels —**Dormir(se) en sus laureles**

right away —**Ahorita; ya; de inmediato; inmediatamente; en seguida** ▪ *I'll tell him right away.* **Le diré en seguida.**

to ring a bell —**Sonar(le)** (familiar: **conocido**) **a (alguien)** ▪ *Sorry. That name doesn't ring a bell.* **Lo siento. Ese nombre no me suena (conocido).**

to rise to the occasion —**Estar (poner(se)) a la altura de las circunstancias**

to risk (to run the risk of) —**Correr riesgos; Correr el riesgo de** (+ verb) ▪ *I'm going to make a note of Fernando's birthday. I know it's still six months away, but I don't want to run the risk of forgetting it.* **Voy a anotar el cumpleaños de Fernando. Ya sé que faltan seis meses, pero no quiero correr el riesgo de que se me olvide.**

to rob (a person or place) —**Asaltar a (alguien o algo); robar (algo)** (from an amateur stickup to a full-scale bank robbery) ▪ *We were robbed.* **Nos asaltaron.** *The two crooks robbed the convenience store.* **Los dos ratas robaron la tiendita.**

to rub shoulders with (someone) —**Codear(se) con (alguien)**

to run a red light —**Pasar(se) el alto**

to run across (someone or something) —**Encontrar(se) (de casualidad) (algo); encontrar(se) a (alguien); topar(se) con (alguien)** ▪ *I ran into Bob at the store.* **Me encontré a (me topé con) Bob en la tienda.**

to run into (someone or something) —**Encontrar(se) (de casualidad) (algo); encontrar(se) a (alguien); topar(se) con (alguien)** to run (someone) out —**Despedir a (alguien);** *(Mex)* (slang) **correr a (alguien); poner de patitas en la calle a (alguien)** ▪ *Mr. Smith ran Pete out of the club.* **El Sr. Smith corrió a Pete del club.** *Adele was run out of the office.* **Despidieron a Adele.**

to run out of (something) —**Acabar(sele) (algo) a (alguien)** ▪ *I've run*

S

to save face —**Guardar las apariencias; no quedar mal** ▪ *I have to do something to save face.* **Tengo que hacer algo para guardar las apariencias (no quedar mal).**

Scram! —**¡Vete! (¡Váyase!; ¡Váyanse!)**

Screw you! —**¡Vete al diablo! (¡Váyanse al diablo!)**

to screw (something) up —**Descomponer (algo); echar a perder (algo)** ▪ *My father screwed up the blender by leaving the spoon in it and turning it on.* **Mi papá descompuso (echó a perder) la licuadora porque la puso a funcionar con la cuchara adentro.** *My sister screwed up the VCR and the tape is stuck.* **Mi hermana descompuso la videograbadora y la cinta está atorada.**

to screw (things) up —**Equivocar(se); meter la pata** *(lit.* to stick your foot in it); (slang) **regar(la)** *(lit.* to spill it) ▪ *Gus was the only one who screwed up.* **Gus fue el único que se equivocó (metió la pata; la regó).**

to screw up the courage to do (something) —**Tener (encontrar) el valor para** (+ verb) ▪ *I just can't screw up the courage to approach him.* **No encuentro el valor para acercarme a él.**

Search me! —*(Mex)* **¿Yo qué sé?; ¡A mí, que me esculquen!**

to see eye to eye about something —**Estar (perfectamente) de acuerdo en (sobre) (algo)** ▪ *I'm glad we see eye to eye on that.* **Qué bueno que estamos de acuerdo en eso.**

to see (someone) off —**Ir a despedir a (alguien)** ▪ *I can't see you off this time.* **Esta vez no puedo ir a despedirte.**

to see (someone) out —**Ir a despedir a (alguien); acompañar a la puerta a (alguien)** ▪ *Can you see me out?* **¿Me acompañas a la puerta?**

to see red —**Enfurecer(se)**

to see that (something) is done —**Encargar(se) de que se haga (algo)**
- *Please see to it that this is sent.* **Por favor encárgate de que esto se envíe.**

to see the handwriting on the wall —**Dar(se) cuenta de lo inevitable**
- *He just doesn't see the handwriting on the wall.* **Simplemente no se da cuenta de lo inevitable.**

See you later. —**Nos vemos al rato.**

to sell (someone) down the river —**Traicionar a (alguien)** ▪ *I didn't know they were going to sell me down the river.* **No sabía que me iban a traicionar.**

to send (someone) to hell —**Mandar al diablo a (alguien); mandar al demonio a (alguien)** ▪ *He doesn't have the guts to send me to hell.* **No tiene el valor para mandarme al diablo.**

to set (someone) up —**Tender(le) una trampa a (alguien)** ▪ *He was set up.* **Le tendieron una trampa.**

to set (something) up —**Establecer; organizar; arreglar; constituir (algo)** (for corporations)

Shit happens. —**A veces las cosas desagradables son inevitables.**

Shove off! —**¡Vete! ¡Lárgate!**

a show of hands —**Votar levantando la mano** ▪ *To save time, we'll just have a show of hands.* **Para no perder tiempo, el voto será levantando la mano.**

to show (something) off —**Lucir (algo); presumir (algo)** ▪ *Now you can show off your new car.* **Ahora puedes lucir tu coche nuevo.**

to show up —**Llegar; aparecer(se)** ▪ *He never showed up.* **Nunca se apareció.**

to shut down —**Cerrar**

to shut (something) off —**Apagar (algo); cortar el suministro de (algo); cerrar(le) a (algo)** ▪ *Shut off the water please.* **Ciérrale al agua por favor.** *They shut off the electricity.* **Cortaron la luz.**

to shut up —**Callar a (alguien); callar(se)**

to sign up for (something) —**Apuntar(se) para (algo); inscribir(se) para (algo)**

to skate on thin ice —**Arriesgar(se); jugar con fuego** (*lit.* to play with fire)

to sleep like a log —**Dormir como tronco** (*lit.* to sleep like a log); **dormir como un lirón** (*lit.* to sleep as if hibernating); **dormir a pierna suelta** to sleep on (something) —**Consultar (algo) con la almohada** ▪ *You don't have to give me an answer right now. Sleep on it.* **No tienes que resolverme ahora. Consúltalo con la almohada.**

small fry —**Niños; chiquillos; bajito(a)** (physical height) (adults); **poca cosa** (insignificance) (things)

so-and-so (so-and-so and so-and-so) —**Fulano (mengano y zutano)** ▪ *No more excuses! According to you, so-and-so said such and such, so-and-so promised God knows what, and so-and-so forced you into something...* **No me vengas con más excusas: que si fulano te dijo, que si mengano te prometió, que si zutano te obligó...**

so far —**Hasta ahora; hasta el día de hoy** ▪ *I plan to live forever. So far, so good.* **Pienso vivir para siempre. Hasta ahora, voy bien.**

So what! —**¡Y qué!**

sooner or later —**Tarde o temprano**

to sow your wild oats —**Andar de picos pardos**

Speaking of the devil ... —**Hablando del rey de Roma ...**

spick-and-span —**Limpio y ordenado; reluciente**

to split hairs —**Discutir pequeñeces**

square meal —**Comida completa** ▪ *Teenagers need three square meals a day.* **Los adolescentes necesitan tres comidas completas al día.**

(a) stab in the back —**Puñalada trapera; puñalada por la espalda**

to stand out —**Sobresalir**

to stand up for (someone or something) —**Salir en defensa de (alguien o algo)** ▪ *I always stand up for my dad.* **Siempre salgo en defensa de mi padre.**

to start at the bottom of the ladder —**Empezar sin nada; empezar desde abajo**

to stay home —**Quedar(se) en casa**

to stay in —**Quedar(se) en casa**

Step on it! —**¡Apúrate!**

to stick around —**No ir(se); quedar(se)** ▪ *I told him to stick around for a while.* **Le dije que se quedara un rato.**

to stick out like a sore thumb —**Ser muy notorio, resaltar; ver(se) mal;** *(Mex)* (slang) **ver(se) de la cachetada**

to stick to —**No apartar(se) de** ▪ *Stick to the main path!* **No se aparten del sendero principal.**

---

to stick up for (someone or something) —**Defender a (alguien o algo)**

to stop at nothing —**Ser capaz de todo; ser capaz de cualquier cosa** ▪ *If Pat really wants something, he stops at nothing.* **Si Pat de veras quiere algo, es capaz de cualquier cosa.**

to stop by —**Dar(se) una vuelta** ▪ *Can you stop by after the game?* **¿Puedes darte una vuelta después del juego?**

to stop (something) cold turkey —**Parar (algo) de golpe; dejar de hacer (algo) de golpe** ▪ *I can't stop smoking cold turkey.* **No puedo dejar el cigarro (de fumar) de golpe.**

straight from the hip —**Francamente; sin rodeos** ▪ *Give it to me straight from the hip.* **Dímelo francamente (sin rodeos).**

stuck-up —**Presumido(a)**

to suit (someone) to a T —**Caer(le) como anillo al dedo a (alguien)** (*lit.* to fit like a ring on a finger) ▪ *This gift suits me to a T.* **Este regalo me cae como anillo al dedo.**

to swallow (something) hook, line and sinker —**Tragar(se) el anzuelo; creer (algo) sin sospechar que es mentira**

Take a flying leap! —**¡Vete a la goma!; ¡Vete al diablo!**

Take a hike! —**¡Vete a la goma!; ¡Vete al diablo!**

to take a leak —**Hacer pipí;** (slang) **hacer del uno**

to take (unfair) advantage of (someone or something) —**Aprovechar(se) de (alguien o algo)** ▪ *He took unfair advantage of the girl.* **Se aprovechó de la muchacha.**

to take after (someone) —**Parecer(se) a (alguien)** ▪ *My baby sister takes after my father.* **Mi hermana menor se parece a mi papá.**

to take (something) apart —**Desarmar (algo)** ▪ *We have to take the carburetor apart.* **Tenemos que desarmar el carburador.**

to take (someone's) breath away —**Dejar atónito a (alguien); dejar boquiabierto a (alguien); dejar con la boca abierta a (alguien)** ▪ *The view of the city took my breath away.* **La vista de la ciudad me dejó atónito (boquiabierto).**

to take care of (someone or something) —**Cuidar (alguien o algo)** ▪ *Take care of your health.* **Cuida tu salud.**

Take care of yourself! —**¡Cuídate!**

to take (something) for granted —**Dar por hecho (algo)** (In Spanish you cannot take a person for granted, only a thing.) ▪ *You had better not take for granted that he is going to come.* **Será mejor que no des por hecho que va a venir.**

to take it easy —**Tomar las cosas con calma**

Take it or leave it. —**Tómalo o déjalo.**

to take off (leave) —**Ir(se)** ▪ *I'm going to take off now, or I'll be late.* **Ya me voy, para no llegar tarde.**

to take over —**Hacer(se) cargo de (algo)** ▪ *Gus took over the department when I left.* **Gus se hizo cargo del departamento cuando me fui.**

to take the bull by the horns —**Agarrar el toro por los cuernos**

to take the cake —**Ser el colmo; llevar(se) la palma** ▪ *This really takes the cake!* **¡Esto realmente es el colmo!**

to take the law into your own hands —**Hacer(se) justicia por su propia mano** ▪ *We might have to take the law into our own hands.* **Quizás tengamos que hacernos justicia por nuestra propia mano.**

to take the prize —**Ser el colmo; llevar(se) la palma**

to take (something) to pieces —**Desarmar (algo)**

to take (someone) to the cleaners —**Perjudicar a (alguien)**; (vulgar) **fregar a (alguien)** ▪ *His wife really took him to the cleaners with the divorce.* **Su esposa realmente lo perjudicó con el divorcio.**

to take turns —**Turnar(se)** ▪ *Let's take turns driving.* **Vamos a turnarnos manejando.**

to take (someone) under your wing —**Tomar bajo su protección a (alguien)** ▪ *He immediately took me under his wing.* **De inmediato me tomó bajo su protección.**

to take (something) up with (someone) —**Tratar (algo) con (alguien); discutir (algo) con (alguien)**

to take (something) with a grain of salt —**Tomar (algo) con reservas** ▪ *Everything Bruce says should be taken with a grain of salt.* **Hay que tomar con reservas todo lo que dice Bruce.**

to take your time —**Tomar(se) su tiempo** ▪ *Don't hurry. Take your time!* **No se apure. ¡Tómese su tiempo!**

to talk a lot of hot air (to talk a lot of bull) —**Hablar tonterías; decir disparates** ▪ *You're talking a lot of hot air.* **Otra vez estás diciendo disparates.**

to talk (someone's) ear off —**Hablar mucho; hablar hasta por los codos** ▪ *Sorry I'm late. I was with Sally and she always talks my ear off.* **Siento llegar tarde. Estaba con Sally, y ella habla hasta por los codos.**

to talk nonsense —**Hablar tonterías; decir disparates**

to talk (something) over —**Hablar (algo); platicar (algo)** ▪ *Let's talk it over.* **Vamos a hablarlo (platicarlo).**

to talk shit —**Hablar mal (echar pestes) de (alguien)** ▪ *I heard she was talking shit about me. Is it true?* **Supe que estuvo hablando mal (echando pestes) de mí. ¿Es cierto?**

to talk turkey —**Hablar sin rodeos**

Tell it to the marines! —**¡A otro perro con ese hueso!**

to tell (someone) off —**Regañar severamente a (alguien); gritar(le) a (alguien)**

That goes without saying. —**No hace falta decirlo.**

That's a horse of a different color. —**Esa es harina de otro costal.**

That's a load of bull! —**¡Esas son patrañas!**

That's another kettle of fish. —**Esa es harina de otro costal;** *(Gua)* **Eso es coche de otro chiquero;** *(Cuba)* **Eso es gallo de otro gallinero.**

That's beside the point. —**Eso no viene al caso.**

That's cold comfort! —**Es un pobre consuelo; ¡Valiente consuelo!**

That's cool! —**¡Qué bueno!**; (slang) **¡Qué suave; ¡Qué padre!**

The coast is clear. —**No hay moros en la costa.**

the latest rage —**El último grito (de la moda)**

the whole enchilada —**Sin que falte nada; por todo lo alto; a todo lujo** ▪ *We want a round-the-world tour with all the trimmings. The whole enchilada.* **Queremos un viaje alrededor del mundo a todo lujo (por todo lo alto).** *She doesn't want a brunch. She wants a seven-course dinner... the whole enchilada.* **Ella no quiere un brunch. Quiere una cena a todo lujo.**

the whole shebang —**Sin que falte nada; por todo lo alto; a todo lujo**

There's no going back. —**Ya no poder echar(se) para atrás.**

There is method in his/her madness. —**Es más cuerdo de lo que parece.**

There is no love lost between them. —**La antipatía es mutua.**

there is no point (+ verb + ing) —**No tiene caso** (+ verb) ▪ *There's no point making lunch. Nobody's hungry.* **No tiene caso hacer de comer. Nadie tiene hambre.**

There's more than meets the eye. —**Aquí hay mar de fondo; aquí hay gato encerrado.**

There's something fishy here. —**Aquí hay gato encerrado.**

to think better of (something) —**Pensar(lo) mejor; cambiar de opinión; cambiar de parecer** ▪ *I've thought better of that plan of yours.* **Cambié de parecer (opinión) acerca de tu plan. (Acerca de tu plan... ya lo pensé mejor.)**

to think highly of (someone or something) —**Tener en gran estima a (alguien o algo); estimar a (alguien o algo); apreciar a (alguien o algo)** ▪ *The manager thinks very highly of you.* **El gerente te tiene en gran estima (te aprecia mucho).**

to think the world of (someone or something) —**Tener en gran estima a (alguien o algo); estimar a (alguien o algo); apreciar a (alguien o algo)**

through the grapevine —**Rumor; chisme** ▪ *I heard it through the grapevine.* **Me lo dijeron como chisme.**

to throw a party —**Hacer una fiesta; ofrecer una fiesta**

to throw (something) away —**Desechar (algo); tirar (algo)** ▪ *Why did you throw away that book?* **¿Por qué tiraste ese libro?**

to throw cold water on (something) —**Echar por tierra (algo)** ▪ *Mr. Harrow threw cold water on the plan.* **El Sr. Harrow echó por tierra el plan.**

to throw in the towel —**Tirar la toalla; dar(se) por vencido** ▪ *If I don't win this round, I'm going to throw in the towel.* **Si no gano esta ronda, voy a tirar la toalla (voy a darme por vencido).**

to throw (someone) out (on their ear) —*(Mex)* (slang) **Correr a (alguien); poner de patitas en la calle a (alguien)**

to throw up —**Vomitar; volver el estómago;** *(Mex)* (slang) **guacarear(se);** *(Mex)* (slang) **cantar Oaxaca**

till you're blue in the face —**Hasta el cansancio; hasta decir basta** ▪ *I warned him about that till I was blue in the face.* **Se lo advertí hasta el cansancio.**

Time's up! —**¡Se acabó el tiempo!**

to tone (something) down —**Bajar(le) el volumen** ▪ *Tone it down guys! The neighbors are going to complain.* **¡Bájenle al volumen! Se van a quejar los vecinos.**

to touch a sore spot —**Poner el dedo en la llaga** ▪ *From her expression, I knew I had touched a sore spot.* **Por su expresión, supe que había puesto el dedo en la llaga.**

to try (something) on —**Probar(se) (algo)** ▪ *Try on this dress.* **Pruébate este vestido.**

to try (something) out —**Probar (algo)** ▪ *Try this out and tell me what you think of it.* **Prueba esto y dime qué te parece.**

to turn a blind eye —**Hacer(se) de la vista gorda** ▪ *Johnny is running around with the wrong crowd, and his father is turning a blind eye.* **Johnny anda con unos tipos indeseables y su padre se hace de la vista gorda.**

to turn around —**Voltear(se); dar(se) la vuelta** ▪ *Turn around and look at me!* **¡Date la vuelta y mírame!**

to turn (someone or something) down —1) **Rechazar (alguien) o (algo)** (to reject) ▪ *I was turned down for the job.* **Me rechazaron para el puesto.** —2) **Negar** (to deny a request) ▪ *They turned down my request.* **Me negaron lo que pedí.**

to turn in —**Ir(se) a la cama; acostar(se)**

to turn (something) off —**Apagar (algo); cortar el suministro de (algo)** to turn out —**Resultar** ▪ *The idea turned out to be excellent.* **La idea resultó ser excelente.**

to turn over a new leaf —**Reformar(se)** ▪ *He has promised to turn over a new leaf.* **Ha prometido reformarse.**

to turn (something) over to (someone) —**Entregar (algo) a (alguien); hacer entrega de (algo) a (alguien)** ▪ *I have to turn the key over to Gordon.* **Tengo que entregarle la llave a Gordon.**

to turn up your nose at (someone or something) —**Despreciar a (alguien o algo);** *(Mex)* (slang) **hacer(le) el fuchi (el feo) a (algo) o a (alguien)** ▪ *Joan turned up her nose at the cake.* **Joan le hizo el fuchi (el feo) al pastel.**

to twist (someone's) arm —**Presionar hasta convencer a (alguien);** *(Mex)* (slang) **hacer(le) manita de puerco a (alguien)** ▪ *Joan doesn't want to go, but I'll twist her arm.* **Joan no quiere ir, pero voy a presionarla (hacerle manita de puerco).**

U

under the table —**Por abajo del agua** ▪ *They pay me a bit more under the table every month.* **Cada mes me pagan un poco más, por abajo del agua.**

to upset the applecart —**Echar(lo) todo a perder; estropear los planes** ▪ *Don't go upsetting the apple cart, for heaven's sake!* **¡No vayas a echar todo a perder, por amor de Dios!**

upside down —**De cabeza** ▪ *The picture is upside down.* **El cuadro está de cabeza.**

used to (+ verb) —**Soler; tener la costumbre de** (+ verb) ▪ *I used to come here all the time.* **Solía (Tenía la costumbre de) venir aquí todo el tiempo.**

to wait on (someone) —**Atender a (alguien)**

to wait on (someone) hand and foot —**Atender a cuerpo de rey a (alguien)** ▪ *They waited on us hand and foot.* **Nos atendieron a cuerpo de rey.**

to wait up for (someone) —**Esperar despierto a (alguien)** ▪ *Don't wait up for me.* **No me esperes despierta.**

to waste your breath —**Perder su tiempo; gastar saliva** ▪ *I could have told you you were wasting your breath. They never listen.* **Te podía haber dicho que estabas perdiendo el tiempo. Ellos no le hacen caso a nadie.**

to wear out —**Desgastar(se)** ▪ *The tires are wearing out.* **Se están desgastando las llantas.**

to wear your heart on your sleeve —**No poder disimular los sentimientos (amorosos)**

What a bummer! —**¡Qué mala suerte!**; (slang) **¡Qué mala pata!**

What do you think you're doing? —**¿Qué haces?; ¿Qué crees que estás haciendo?**

What nerve! —**¡Qué poca vergüenza!**

What's new? —**¿Qué hay de nuevo?**

What's up? —**¿Qué hay de nuevo?**

wild-goose chase —**Búsqueda inútil, infructuosa** ▪ *You sent me out on another wild-goose chase.* **Me mandaste a otra búsqueda inútil.**

with flying colors —**Con gran éxito**

with your hands tied behind your back —**Con la mano en la cintura** ▪ *I can beat you at tennis with my hands tied behind my back.* **Te gano al tenis con la mano en la cintura.**

without batting an eye —**Sin pestañear**

without rhyme or reason —**Sin ton ni son** ▪ *Your brother argues without rhyme or reason.* **Tu hermano discute sin ton ni son.**

(a) wolf in sheep's clothing —**Lobo con piel de oveja**

to work (something) out —**Solucionar (algo); buscar una solución a (algo)** ▪ *We have to work this out with Ian.* **Tenemos que buscar una solución al problema junto con Ian.**

to work your way up —**Abrir(se) paso; abrir(se) camino** ▪ *He worked his way up to where he is now in only five years.* **En sólo cinco años se abrió paso (camino) hasta lo que es ahora.**

to wrap (someone) around your little finger —**Tener dominado(a) a (alguien); traer marcando el paso a (alguien); traer cortito(a) a (alguien)**

You can tell … —**Se nota que …** ▪ *You can tell he's tired.* **Se nota que está cansado.**

You can't miss it! —**¡No tiene pierde!** ▪ *Turn right at the corner and you will find the house in the middle of the block. You can't miss it!* **En la esquina das vuelta a la derecha y encuentras la casa a mitad de la cuadra. ¡No tiene pierde!**

You don't say! —**¡No me digas!**

You should know better than that. —**Estás haciendo algo que sabes que no debes hacer.**

Index

A

A big stink, 20, 66
A big to-do, 52, 53, 83
A lot, 20, 30, 65
A must, 9, 46
Abandon, 39
Absolutely!, 105
Accuse of, 25
Act of drinking, 30
Act of God, 24, 105
Act of necking, 53
Act of taking advantage, 18
Act senile, 30
Act the same way as, 77
Add fuel to the fire, 42, 105
Add insult to injury, 24, 79, 105
Adults, old people, 67
After all, 14, 40
Aggressive, 12
Air your dirty laundry in public,
   105
All his or her bulk, 26
All of a sudden, 105
All the livelong day, 95
Allow yourself to be impressed, 16
All-time high, 105
Amusing, 98
Angry, 15
Announcement of a candidate for
   a government position, 40
Anyway, 14, 37
Apparently, 14
Appear to be fervently religious, 34
Appear to be a certain age, 17
Are you kidding?, 105
As a matter of fact, 105
As is, 93
As it is, 38
As soon as, 44
As the crow flies, 45, 105
As usual, 105
Ask for it, 85, 105
Ask someone to do something, 45
Ask the impossible, 75
At about, 9
At last, 105
At least, 105

At once, 105
At the beginning of, 10
At the drop of a hat, 105
At the end of, 9
At the ends of the earth, 44
At the latest, 10
At this point of the game, 9
At whatever cost, 11
Avoid getting involved, 99
Avoid someone, 57

B

Babble, 55
Bad, badly, 38
Bad language, 75
Bad luck, 64
Badly dressed person, 58
Badmouth, 43, 55, 106
Bar, 29
Barely, 9
Barf, 106
Bathing suit, 22
Bawl out, 106
Bawl the hell out of someone, 42
Be a bastard, 91
Be a big fish in a small pond,
   87, 106
Be a bit drunk, 47
Be a bone of contention, 88, 106
Be a bottomless pit of wisdom, 90
Be a busybody, 87, 89, 106
Be a despicable person, 90
Be a drunkard, 89
Be a dull person on the surface,
   89, 90
Be a far cry from, 49, 106
Be a feather in your cap, 106
Be a fine figure of a man, 89
Be a foul-mouthed person, 89
Be a gigolo, 90
Be a good person, 90
Be a good student, 89
Be a goody two-shoes, 88
Be a goody-goody, 88
Be a great guy, 87, 106
Be a helper, 90

Beat around the bush, 15, 16, 112
Beat someone hands down, 112
Beat someone up, 64, 92
Become disheartened, 13
Become inhibited, 12
Become intimidated, 11
Become listless and dispirited, 17
Become or look old, 34
Become something, 63
Become strict, 78
Become very sad, 12
Beer, 24, 28
Bend over backwards, 67
Better half, 65, 112
Better not, 112
Big, 30
Big shot, 64, 112
Big stink, 20
Big to-do, 52, 53, 83
Bite off more than you can chew, 65, 112
Bite someone's head off, 112
Black coffee, 22
Blond, 24, 54, 64
Blow it, 112
Blow money, 97
Blow off steam, 113
Blow one's own horn, 113
Blow something, 97, 112
Blow the whistle, 34
Blow your nose, 92
Blow your top, 113
Boast, 25, 32
Boastful loudmouth, 28, 42, 52
Boot someone out, 113
Bother, 45, 52, 61, 64, 76
Bounce, 83
Bowlegged, 30
Boy, 28, 53, 76
Boy, girl, 28, 75
Brawl, 13
Break down, 40, 113
Break the ice, 113
Break up with someone, 97
Bribe, 19, 24, 36, 75, 95, 98
Bring a person under control, 66
Bring home the bacon, 113

Bring someone down a few notches, 19
Brownnose, 113
Brownnoser, 62
Bucks, 98
Bug, 113
Bull!, 113
Bullshit!, 10
Bunch of something, 20
Bundle of clothes, 93
Burn …, 12
Burn the candle at both ends, 113
Burn the midnight oil, 82
Burn your bridges behind you, 113
Bury the hatchet, 57, 113
Bury your head in the sand, 113
Bus, 53
Bust a gut, 113
Busybody, 29
Butt in, 65
Butter up, 32
Buy a pig in a poke, 113
By chance, 37, 38
By leaps and bounds, 10, 113
By myself, 113
By the skin of your teeth, 114
By the way, 11, 114
By very little, 79
Bye-bye, 12

C

Call a spade a spade, 63, 115
Call it quits!, 14
Call off, 115
Call someone all the names in the book, 115
Call the shots, 115
Cannon fodder, 23
Car, 24, 68
Careful!, 11, 20
Carelessly, 9, 14
Caress, 12, 16, 17
Carry out, 115
Catch an illness, 76
Catch someone, 13, 21, 35, 76, 97

G

Get strict, 52
Get stubborn, 67
Get stuck, 123
Get the hang of, 45, 123
Get the short end of the stick, 85
Get the show on the road, 123
Get too big for your boots, 123
Get up on the wrong side of the
  bed, 62, 123
Get up the guts to do, 56
Get upset, 56, 92
Get uptight, 12
Get used to, 123
Get used to the idea, 55
Get with it, 123
Gift, 27
Girl, 29
Girl in love, 53
Give a hand, 123
Give a hard time, 23, 123
Give a nasty feeling, 35
Give a piece of your mind,
  23, 29, 123
Give a ride, 36, 124
Give a ring, 43, 124
Give a taste of his own medicine,
  36, 124
Give a terrific blow, 36
Give a wide berth, 124
Give birth, 15, 32
Give directions, 36
Give food for thought, 34
Give free rein, 124
Give hell, 124
Give him an inch, and he'll take a
  mile, 124
Give in, 40, 124
Give it a rest!, 124
Give me a break!, 124
Give moral support, 32
Give someone what he's got
  coming to him, 125
Give something a good go, 32
Give something a rest, 37
Give the cold shoulder, 124
Give the creeps, 33, 35, 78
Give the once-over, 66

Give the shaft, 124
Give the slip, 124
Give up, 30, 35, 83, 124, 125
Give walking papers, 125
Give your all, 125
Give yourself away, 35
Go against the grain, 125
Go all out, 95, 125
Go around the bend, 125
Go back on your word, 29, 83
Go bother someone else, 59
Go crazy, 125
Go fly a kite!, 125
Go from bad to worse, 59, 125
Go in a great hurry, 60
Go into a great deal of confusing
  detail, 43
Go it alone, 125
Go jump in the lake, 59, 66, 125
Go lickety-split, 60, 99
Go like a streak, 60
Go nuts, 125
Go on a binge, 125
Go on a drinking spree, 59
Go on the wagon, 125
Go out with, go steady, 85
Go over, 125
Go overboard, 70
Go shopping, 59
Go slowly, 59
Go the whole hog, 42
Go through hell, 75
Go to town, 126
Go too far, 64, 74
Go under, 126
Go with, 126
Gofer, 23
Good, elegant, 28
Good Lord!, 81
Good-looking woman, 101
Goof off, 126
Gosh!, 44, 58
Gossip, senseless talk, 53
Gossipy, 20, 22
Got it!, 101
Grease someone's palm, 126
Great!, 11

Grudge, 24
Guessing what time it is, 55
Guitar, 73
Guy, 58
Gyp or deceive, 34

H

Had better, 127
Hand in, 127
Handsome, good-looking person, 31
Hang around, 127
Hangover, 27, 53, 83
Haphazardly, 14
Have a bone to pick with, 127
Have a chip on your shoulder, 127
Have a date, 95
Have a fit, 33, 34, 127
Have a go at it!, 63
Have a good time, 127
Have a green thumb, 127
Have a hangover, 48
Have a hard time, 92, 92
Have a hunch, 62, 64, 127
Have a lot of nerve, 87, 93
Have a lot of smarts, 86
Have a lot on the ball, 127
Have a lump in your throat, 127
Have a mean streak, 94
Have a mess, 95
Have a pleasant personality, 94
Have a poker face, 77
Have a screw loose, 127
Have a shot (a drink), 43, 44
Have a silver lining, 95
Have a smattering of knowledge, 95
Have a soft spot, 49, 127
Have a sweetheart, 95
Have a tantrum, 57
Have a terrible time, 74
Have a voice in, 128
Have an ax to grind, 128
Have an intense confrontation, 36
Have bad luck, 22
Have bats in the belfry, 128
Have enough, 95, 128

Have guts, 128
Have irons in the fire, 128
Have its cons, 95
Have no choice, 128
Have no gumption, 94
Have on your mind, 94, 128
Have one too many, 74, 128
Have pull, 94, 95
Have sex, 44
Have sex before marriage, 25, 66
Have skeletons in the closet, 93
Have small change, 94
Have someone figured out, 128
Have someone in stitches, 93
Have someone on a short leash, 96
Have someone's number, 128
Have something done, 128
Have something figured out, 128
Have something to eat on the go, 44
Have something unpleasant happen, 59
Have spunk, 128
Have the answer, 85
Have the capacity to take negative acts/nonsense, 13
Have the gift of gab, 129
Have the runs, 48, 94
Have to do with, 128
Have too many, 50
Have unbreakable integrity, 88
Have very little, 69
Have your hands full with, 129
Have your heart in the right place, 129
He doesn't eat enough to feed a bird, 129
He's every inch a man, 129
Head, 24, 29, 30, 64
Hear from, 129
Help yourself, 129
Helper, 12
He-man, 64
Hit pay dirt, 129
Hit the ceiling, 24, 74, 129
Hit the hay, 129
Hit the nail on the head, 32, 34, 129

P

Pack your bags, 141
Pain in the neck, 62, 67, 76
Painful fall, 83
Paint the town red, 84
Panties, 30
Parcel, 20
Park, 74
Parking lot, 74
Parsimony, 73
Party, 20, 84
Pay attention, 55
Pay attention!, 32
Pay for, 32
Pay lip service to, 141
Pay no attention, 39
Pay through the nose, 73, 141
Pay up, 17, 21
Pay up!, 22
Pee, 55
Penny for your thoughts, 141
Perhaps, 10
Perk up, 78
Person frying fast food, 30
Person of loose morals, 27
Person or thing from the United
    States, 53
Person who always mooches off
    others, 53
Person who backs out of a deal, 83
Person who feels up a woman, 18
Person who goes back on his
    word, 87
Person who handles legal
    procedures, 27
Person who installs and fixes gas
    heaters, 53
Person who is a pest, 52
Person who is crass, vulgar, 68
Person who is rushing around
    ineffectually, 87
Person who is the best at, 52
Person who makes others waste
    time, 87
Person who rarely gets anything
    right, 28
Person who stutters, 53

Person who sucks up, 87
Person who takes advantage, 17, 18
Person who talks too much, 58
Person with a lot of nerve, 26
Person with an attractive body, 97
Person with no feelings of guilt, 87
Petty thief, 83
Pick a quarrel, 141
Pick up the tab, 141
Piece of cake, 73
Pig, 28
Pious Catholic, 66, 67
Pipe down!, 141
Piss off, 141
Pitch in together, 43
Play a dirty trick on someone, 91
Play around, 141
Play ball, 61, 141
Play dead, 141
Play down, 141
Play dumb, 55, 56, 141
Play hard to get, 56, 141
Play hooky, 59, 141
Play it cool, 12, 141
Play it safe, 141
Play practical jokes, 97
Play the …, 141
Play the big shot, 141
Play the horses, 142
Play with fire, 61
Pleasantly, 38
Plot against someone, 67
Point out, 78
Policeman, 21, 73
Poor luck, 28
Pop in on someone, 142
Pour oil on the fire, 142
Practical joke, 21
Praise to the skies, 77
Prejudice against (to), 22
Pressure to do fast (to), 23
Pretend, 33, 55, 56, 73
Pretend to be reluctant, 57
Promise the Earth, 80, 142
Properly, correctly, 25
Pug-nosed, 28
Pull a fast one, 142

Wander, 98
Want to beat up or kill someone, 96
Want to bet?, 11
Want to get someone into bed, 96
Warn, 42
Waste someone's time, 45
Waste your breath, 154
Watch or clock, fast, 47
Watch out!, 13, 14
Way to go!, 13
Wear out, 154
Wear your heart on your sleeve, 154
Weigh a ton, 76
Well!, 98
What!, 25
What a bore!, 81
What a bummer!, 154
What a faux pas!, 81
What a pain!, 81
What a scream!, 81
What a shame!, 64
What do you think of that?, 58
What do you think you're doing?, 154
What luck!, 81
What nerve!, 81, 154
What with one thing and another, 46
What's new?, 81, 154
What's up?, 154
When pigs fly, 27
When something comes naturally, 68
When the going gets tough, 9
When the time comes, 9
Who knows!, 11
Whole lot, 83, 95
Whorehouse, 82
Wild-goose chase, 154
Willingly, 37
Win by making others look ridiculous, 73
With all one's might and main, 10
With flying colors, 154
With great difficulty, 26

With great effort, 26
With the greatest of ease, 26
With your hands tied behind your back, 154
Without any trimmings, 11
Without batting an eye, 154
Without rhyme or reason, 92, 154
Without warning, 37, 91
Witty, 27
Wolf in sheep's clothing, 154
Wonderfully well, 10, 38
Work, 28, 97
Work hard, 12, 23, 52
Work oneself up, 33
Work something out, 154
Work up speed, 13
Work your way up, 154
Worry, 48
Worthless person, 75
Wrap around your finger, 93, 94, 155

Y

Yell, 75
Yes?, 65
You can tell, 155
You can't miss it!, 155
You don't say!, 155
You should know better than that, 155
You-know-what, 17
You-know-who, 17
Young people, 28
Youngster, 46
You're welcome, 69

Z

Zero, 68

Spanish and Latin American Interest Titles
from Hippocrene Books

LANGUAGE GUIDES

Spanish-English/English-Spanish Practical Dictionary
35,000 ENTRIES • 338 PAGES • 5 X 8 • 0-7818-0179-6 • $9.95PB • (211)

Spanish-English/English-Spanish Concise Dictionary
(Latin American)
8,000 ENTRIES • 500 PAGES • 4 X 6 • 0-7818-0261-X • $11.95PB • (258)

Hippocrene Children's Illustrated Spanish Dictionary
English-Spanish/Spanish-English
500 ENTRIES • 94 PAGES • 8 X 11 • 0-7818-0733-6 • $14.95HC • (206)

Beginner's Spanish
313 PAGES • 5 1/2 X 8 1/2 • 0-7818-0840-5 • $14.95PB • (225)

Mastering Spanish
338 PAGES • 5 X 8 • 0-87052-059-8 • $11.95PB • (527)
2 CASSETTES: CA. 2 HOURS • 0-87052-067-9 • $12.95 • (528)

Mastering Advanced Spanish
326 PAGES • 5 X 8 • 0-7818-0081-1 • $14.95PB • (413)
2 CASSETTES: CA. 2 HOURS • 0-7818-0089-7 • $12.95 • (426)

Spanish Grammar
224 PAGES • 5 X 8 • 0-87052-893-9 • $12.95PB • (273)

Spanish Verbs: Ser and Estar
220 PAGES • 5 X 8 • 0-7818-0024-2 • $8.95PB • (292)

Dictionary of 1,000 Spanish Proverbs: Bilingual
131 PAGES • 5 X 8 • 0-7818-0412-4 • $11.95PB • (254)

Spanish Proverbs, Idioms and Slang
350 PAGES • 6 X 9 • 0-7818-0675-5 • $14.95PB • (760)

Basque-English/English-Basque Dictionary and Phrasebook
1,500 ENTRIES • 240 PAGES • 3 X 7 • 0-7818-0622-4 • $11.95PB • (751)

Catalan-English/English-Catalan Concise Dictionary
9,000 ENTRIES • 224 PAGES • 4 X 6 • 0-7818-0099-4 • $9.95PB • (451)

Galician-English/English-Galician Concise Dictionary
10,000 ENTRIES • 600 PAGES • 4 X 6 • 0-7818-0776-X • $14.95PB • (58)

Portuguese-English/English-Portuguese Practical Dictionary
3,000 ENTRIES • 426 PAGES • 4 X 7 • 0-87052-980-3 • $19.95PB • (477)

HISTORY

Mexico: An Illustrated History
150 PAGES • 5 X 7 • 50 ILLUSTRATIONS • 0-7818-0690-9 • $11.95PB • (585)

Spain: An Illustrated History
175 PAGES • 5 X 7 • 50 B/W PHOTOS/ILLUS./MAPS • 0-7818-0874-X • $12.95PB • (339)

Tikal: An Illustrated History of the Ancient Maya Capital
271 PAGES • 6 X 9 • 50 B/W PHOTOS/ILLUS./MAPS • 0-7818-0853-7 • $14.95PB • (101)

BILINGUAL POETRY

Treasury of Spanish Love Poems, Quotations and Proverbs: Bilingual
128 PAGES • 5 X 7 • 0-7818-0358-6 • $11.95 • (589)
2 CASSETTES: CA. 2 HOURS • $12.95 • (584) • 0-7818-0365-9

Treasury of Spanish Love Short Stories in Spanish and English
157 PAGES • 5 X 7 • 0-7818-0298-9 • $11.95 • (604)

COOKBOOKS

Argentina Cooks!: Treasured Recipes from the Nine Regions of Argentina
300 PAGES • 6 X 9 • 0-7818-0829-4 • $24.95HC • (85)

Cuisines of Portuguese Encounters
260 PAGES • 6 X 9 • 0-7818-083106 • $24.95HC • (91)

Old Havana Cookbook (Bilingual)
Cuban Recipes in Spanish and English
128 PAGES • 5 X 7 • ILLUSTRATIONS • 0-7818-0767-0 • $11.95HC • (590)

A Spanish Family Cookbook, Revised Edition
244 PAGES • 5 X 8 • 0-7818-0546-5 • $11.95PB • (642)

Art of South American Cookery
266 PAGES • 5 X 8 • B/W LINE DRAWINGS • 0-7818-0485-X • $11.95PB • (423)

The Art of Brazilian Cookery
240 PAGES • 5 1/2 X 8 1/2 • 0-7818-0130-3 • $11.95PB • (250)

Prices subject to change without prior notice. To order Hippocrene Books, contact your local bookstore, call (718) 454-2366, visit www.hippocrenebooks.com, or write to: Hippocrene Books, 171 Madison Avenue, New York, NY 10016. Please enclose check or money order adding $5.00 shipping (UPS) for the first book and $.50 for each additional title.